i

Praise for Water Yourself

Water Yourself is an amazingly inspirational, easy to follow step-by-step guide to changing your life. Shannon stresses the importance of self-care as the basis for lifelong and sustainable change. The book is peppered with personal and sometimes hilarious anecdotes from Shannon's own experiences that demonstrate her authenticity and charm. I recommend this book to anyone looking to make life changes by taking small steps that lead to major transformations of the mind and body.

Nichole Malkiel, Health Coach & Personal Trainer

Shannon's informal style makes this book an easy read but it's packed with information. It's a step-by-step guide to becoming your best self. I'm so glad I read it!

Mary Columbo Reichert

Dedication

I'd like to dedicate this book to a few women who have moved me and have an indelible place in my heart.

First, to my friend "Slapper," the beautiful princess who inspired me - and this book - in many ways. Thank you for opening your heart and sharing your light.

Second, to my dear friend Nita who left this world much too soon. Her light burned brightly and her infectious energy filled each room, and everyone within it, with exuberance and joy.

Finally, to my lifelong friend and "wind beneath my wings" (you know who you are). You are filled with so much talent and beauty. Don't ever let the world take that from you.

Table of Contents

Foreword

I met Shannon over a year ago when she asked me to be a speaker on one of her events. Since our connection, I have found Shannon to be very creative, innovative and extremely attentive to detail. She has proven to be very professional no matter what setting she is in.

Shannon is a true inspiration to people, especially women. She has taken her life experiences and turned them into creative ways to uplift, encourage and motivate. She brings excitement and love to everything that she touches. I am honored to be her friend and Spiritual Mother.

In "Water Yourself" she gives women a real sense of why self-care is so important. She paints a clear picture and roadmap of how-to self-care. I think because we as women typically take care of everyone else but ourselves, Every Woman needs this book in their Library. Shannon is a blessing to women all over the world, most definitely me.

Dr. Jacqueline King
CEO/Founder Black Women Empowered

The Birth of Watering

"As you grow older, you will realize that
you have two hands, one for helping yourself,
the other for helping others."

Maya Angelou

I guess the best way to tell you about the birth of watering is to start from the beginning. As with all good stories, this one started with a beautiful princess in distress, and I was lucky enough, blessed really, to be part of this fairy tale.

The woman I speak of came into my life through a mutual friend. We saw each other at group gatherings, dinners and parties, but we never really spent any time together one-on-one. Although I knew her, I didn't really *know* her. Our conversations were usually brief and along the lines of one you'd have with a business associate or acquaintance.

"Hi, how are you?"
"Great, you?"
"Wonderful! What's new?"
"Same old, same old. Work. Taking care of my son."
[We look at obligatory cute kid pictures.]
"Oh, he's getting so big! What a cutie...."

It was your typical making conversation and then moving on to the next person in the room type of thing. It wasn't that she wasn't nice, because she was, or that I didn't want to get to know her, because I did, but the party atmosphere and large group situations just weren't ever really conducive to deeper connection.

Our relationship carried along in this manner for years. But then one day, something changed – she began to confide in me. I'm not quite sure why. Maybe I was in the right place at the right time when she needed a friendly ear. Perhaps she just wanted the advice of someone that wasn't close to her situation – someone who could provide a different perspective. Or maybe it's because I'm an empath and possess that "energy" that lets people know I provide a safe, nonjudgmental place for them to come and share their woes (in high school my friends called me 'Shrink Shannon'). Whatever the reason, I'm glad she did.

She started to talk with me about some tough things she was going through, most prominently a divorce, but also some health and overall wellbeing issues. At first, all I provided was an empathetic ear and supportive words. But the more she talked, the more it was clear to me that I could really help her. At that time I was doing health and lifestyle coaching, and I shared with her that I felt I could help her with some of the heath and mindset things she was struggling with. She said she'd think about it.

About a week later, she reached out and said she wanted to work with me on getting over her anxiety so she could get to a happier and healthier place for herself and her son. Her anxiety had become so bad that she was having multiple anxiety attacks every day and it was affecting her ability to do her job and function in general. Sleeping had become nearly impossible because her brain was riddled with thoughts of the divorce, and she was consumed by sadness. She would lie awake most nights thinking about what she did wrong or what she could have done differently to keep her marriage together. And if she wasn't thinking she was crying.

Her life had become a never-ending cycle of anxiety and sadness, and she felt as if she would never regain her happiness. Worst of all, she had started to accept this as her new normal; that this would be her life from this point on.

I knew that to effectively help her achieve her health and life goals, I needed to get to know her better. What made her happy? Sad? Stressed? Angry? Anxious? What were her obstacles and blockers? Motivators? Interests?

After just a few short sessions, I learned that she is an absolutely amazing and incredibly talented woman. She is creative, artistic, selfless, smart...a veritable superwoman. The more I got to know her, the more in awe I was. Here was this woman who had so much to offer, but she didn't see or realize it. She was defining herself by one thing, a failed marriage. Her husband had left her and she became so consumed by it – and by him – that she couldn't see anything else. She discounted her talents, and, even worse, felt she was unimportant and undeserving of love.

As we went through our sessions, one of the most astounding things I discovered is her unrelenting ability to see the good in others. Here she was, struggling through a divorce yet not speaking ill of her ex, something very rare for someone devastated by heartbreak. In fact, she did quite the opposite. She spoke of what a wonderful father he is and how she wanted to continue to have a friendship with him to ensure their son grew up with a mother and father in an environment where he didn't have to split time between them. She wanted to focus on the good of her new situation, but couldn't quite seem to overcome despair to see how fantastically she could thrive on her own.

As the picture started to come together, I was able to gain clarity on how I could better help her overcome and get her life back. During our first session I had provided her with a book on anxiety relief techniques and suggested meditation and other common anxiety-reducing activities. She was incorporating some of the suggestions, but with limited success. I would provide new suggestions each week, techniques from books I had read and research I had done, but she still saw limited results.

As time went on, I realized that I needed to do something more, something different. Traditional methods weren't working, so I needed to reach deep down and come up with a way to help her see what I saw – a beautiful, smart and incredibly talented woman with a plethora to offer the world. And not only see it, *believe* it. Only then would she start to recognize her self-worth. Only then would she start taking care of herself. She spent so much time looking after and taking care of others that she let her own happiness and wellbeing fall to the wayside. I needed a plan, a technique for helping her to bring herself – her wellbeing, goals and aspirations – to the forefront; to help her foster self-love. And that's when Water Yourself was born.

The woman I speak of is just like so many others in the world, maybe even you. Our innate longing to nurture leads us to spend countless hours worrying about and caring for others while neglecting to spend much needed time and energy taking care of ourselves.

I developed Water Yourself to help one very special woman overcome a devastating and life-changing event, find the beauty and love within herself, and harness the courage to accept and be who she is. As I coached more individuals, I realized that there are countless others out there who can benefit from watering themselves; I just needed a way to share it with them. That's why I decided to sit down and write this book, so that I can bring this simple, yet effective, set of principles to those who need it.

Since first publishing Water Yourself in 2014, it has been read in ten countries and I have received heartwarming messages from readers sharing life-changing results and successful outcomes they have achieved by implementing the principles and advice herein. This book also inspired a program for young women called the "Garden Club".

In the first edition of this book I wrote, "...if this book and the content within can help just one person, then my mission is accomplished (although I hope to help so many more)." I am elated to know that it is helping and inspiring people around the world.

So read on, plant a seed and don't forget to Water Yourself!

Water Yourself

"Don't judge each day by the harvest you reap
but by the seeds that you plant."

Robert Louis Stevenson

You've read it a number of times already, but what does it actually mean to Water Yourself? Watering yourself, put simply, is self-care. It's the act of devoting time to and taking care of yourself so that you can accomplish your goals and dreams, and experience personal growth, health and happiness.

It could be something as simple as taking an hour away from it all to breathe and relax. Getting a massage or mani/pedi. Reading a book that you've been wanting to read, but just haven't been able to find the time. Going to a movie with friends, for a hike or to the gym. In the most basic sense, watering yourself is taking the time to invest in yourself by doing something that you enjoy.

But watering yourself goes beyond simple joys and relaxation. It is also a way to advance your personal growth and development, improve your mental and spiritual wellbeing, and enhance your health and happiness. It's doing more than just rewarding yourself; it's **investing in yourself**. Watering yourself enables you to unlock possibilities by opening your mind and expanding your horizons. You could do this by learning something new, visiting a place you've never been or exposing yourself to people, cultures and/or experiences that are completely unknown to you.

Just as a plant needs to be watered regularly to keep from withering and to promote growth, you need to do the same.

But it's not always easy to remember to water yourself. Life and its priorities, along with our innate tendency to put others' needs first, manage to override our personal needs. I'm not talking about our basic needs; self-preservation wins out in those cases. I'm talking about our needs for living our purpose and experiencing fulfillment and joy. That's why I developed the watering system.

The Watering System
As you undoubtedly know, water is vital to a plant's survival. Whether you have a single houseplant or a full-fledged garden, you know and understand the importance of regularly watering a plant. Plants that go without water begin to wilt and wither, then eventually die. **You are no different.** Plants just show their signs and symptoms much quicker and more obviously than we do. Just because you don't necessarily see the results that a lack of watering has on you, it doesn't mean you aren't experiencing the effects of not being watered.

So here's the bottom line – plants need to be watered regularly for growth and survival. We need to be watered regularly for fulfillment, growth and happiness. And since we have a tendency to better remember to water our plants than ourselves, this simple system will remind you to water yourself regularly. Are you ready? Wait for it...here it is:

Water your plant. Water yourself.

Wait, what? Yes, it's really that simple. Each time you water your plant, let that serve as a reminder to water yourself. Here are step-by-step instructions for watering:

1. Pick a plant that you own. Any plant. If you don't have a plant, go buy one. And if you're worried about having a plant because you have a brown thumb and struggle to keep them alive, try some kind of succulent or cactus; they're relatively easy to keep alive.
2. Put the plant in a place where you'll see it every single day (and, of course, where it will get the proper amount of sunlight). This way you can't forget about it, and it will serve as a daily reminder to take care of it <u>and yourself</u>.
3. Now, every time you water your plant, you should water yourself. I'm not talking about taking the watering can and drenching yourself from head to toe (although that *would* be funny to watch). I'm talking about rewarding yourself, finding your happy place, doing something nice for yourself, investing in yourself, and, most importantly, making time for yourself.

Easy right? **Water your plant. Water yourself.** I guarantee that every time you water a plant from this point forward, you will remember to do something for yourself. Whether you actually do it or not is up to you, but I certainly hope you will.

I had a client who only had one plant when I taught her about watering herself. Within a few weeks, she was feeling so great she went out and bought another plant so that she could water more often, because watering herself increased her happiness and decreased her stress.

I had another client who had no plants. She claimed to have a "black thumb" and said she couldn't have a plant because it would surely die – so I went out and bought her two plants (just in case one didn't make it). I told her to put them in a place where she'd see them every day. As I checked in with her to see how the plants were doing and how her watering was going, I was happy to learn that the plants were still living, and, even more importantly, she was thriving. Pretty powerful stuff when you think about it!

Now, it's important to keep in mind that there *is* such a thing as overwatering. We all know what happens to a plant when it gets too much water – it can droop, roots can rot, and it can even die. It doesn't hurt to water regularly, since making time for yourself on a daily basis is a good thing, but don't use watering as an excuse to saturate your life with unfulfilling things (e.g., too many shopping trips and meaningless objects), because in the end those things will only leave you feeling empty. **Watering yourself should be used as way to enrich and better your life.**

Watering Tools

In this section you will find tools to help you water yourself and track your progress.

Watering Log

Use the **Watering Log** at the end of this chapter to track your waterings. Record the date you water yourself, what you do and how it makes you feel.

As time goes on, you should pay attention to how different watering activities make you feel. Which watering activities provide a short-term boost in mood? Which are deeper and longer lasting? The goal is to figure out which activities are most impactful and meaningful. Then, as you experience life's seasons (the ups and downs we all go through), you'll be able to reference your **Watering Log** to understand which activities helped you feel a certain way, and employ the watering activity that best helps you weather the season you're in.

Growth Tracker

As you track your waterings, you should also track your growth. This will help you see the effects that watering has on you. Why is this important?

Have you ever tried to lose weight, tone up or even grow your hair out? If you're like most women, the answer to that question is yes. And if you're a man, replace "tone up" with "beef up" and "grow your hair out" with "grow your beard out." I bet the answer is still yes. Because we look at ourselves in the mirror every single day, it becomes difficult for us to notice slow and subtle changes without some kind of benchmark or tracking tool such as weight, measurements or before and after pictures.

Watering yourself is no different. **It's easy to lose sight of how far we've come when we don't have a benchmark for where we've been.** The Growth Tracker is a way to take a snapshot in time by recording how you feel and keeping sight of your goals and dreams. You then have a way to look back at the progress you've made and see how far you've come.

When considering your **goals**, document things that are specific and measurable. For example, "I want to write and publish a book by the end of the year."

Dreams, on the other hand, are less concrete. A dream may be something like, "I want to be a best-selling author." Think of goals as the steps you need to achieve in order to make your dreams a reality.

In the example I provided, writing and publishing a book would be goals that need to be accomplished before becoming a best-selling author (you can't be a best-selling author without a book).

Approach goals in steps. It's much easier to accomplish goals by breaking them down into smaller, easier to attain milestones than tackling them as lofty, and often seemingly unachievable, goals. Breaking your goals down into smaller, more achievable milestones will not only provide you with a sense of accomplishment as you conquer each one, but it will keep you motivated and moving along the right path toward achieving your larger goals and, eventually, your dreams.

Sticking with the 'writing a book' example - you might set larger, quarterly milestones with smaller monthly and weekly milestones. Each of these milestones should be SMART (Specific, Measurable, Attainable, Realistic and Timely (have a deadline/timeline).

For example, you may have a goal to complete writing of the first draft of the book in 3 months. If your book contains 12 chapters, then you'll need to write 4 chapters each month. That could then be broken down to completing 1 chapter each week.

As you can see, this approach makes achieving your goal more specific, measurable and attainable than if you solely focused on the goal of 'write a book.'

Don't forget to celebrate your wins along the way! Each time you complete a milestone, make sure to acknowledge your achievements. This will keep you motivated and moving toward your goal. Before you know it, that big goal will be accomplished!

So what are you waiting for!? Get started toward accomplishing your dreams by setting your goals, developing milestones and tracking your progress using the **Growth Tracker** at the end of this chapter.

Apply Accountability
Accountability is a great way to stay on track with watering and accomplishing your goals. Here are a couple of ways to help you hold yourself accountable for watering yourself regularly or working toward your goals.

Expand your garden. Teaming up with family members, significant others, friends or colleagues who are also watering and/or working toward goals can serve as an additional level of reinforcement to remind you to water or make sure you hit your milestones. It can also strengthen your bond with one another.

Here are some ways you can water yourself with others: go on a picnic, watch a movie, go out to dinner, go for a hike, enroll in a class, attend a conference, go on a retreat...the possibilities are endless. Sharing experiences with loved ones can also boost the watering experience.

Explore new gardens. Share your watering pride with the world! Take a picture watering yourself and post it to your Facebook, Twitter, Instagram, Pinterest, or other social media, and add #wateryourself. You'll be sharing your watering experiences with a community of like-minded individuals who are doing the same thing. Through this process you'll be introduced to an external support group where you can find a wealth of valuable resources and may even meet new friends. Studies have shown that people who do things in a group are more successful than those who go it alone.

Search #wateryourself on social media to see how others are watering themselves, encourage them to continue, and get new watering ideas for yourself.

Make Time to Water

It's one thing to remind yourself to water, but a whole different ball game to actually incorporate it into your life. **Many people tell me they just don't have time for self-care or feel guilty when they utilize their free time for themselves instead of others.** Well guess what...

Self-care is not selfish!

In fact, when you make the time to care for yourself and recharge your batteries, you're better equipped to care for others. **Remember: You can't pour from an empty cup.**

The truth is you DO have time for yourself, you're just not making it. Prioritizing your own health and happiness, especially in the hustle-bustle world we live in, has fallen by the wayside.

The first step to reaping the benefits of watering yourself is to make time for it, and the only way to do that is to make yourself a priority.

One of the biggest priority changes I encourage people to make revolves around work. We've become so accustomed to staying late and working through our lunch hour that it has become the new norm. It's no longer considered staying late to work an hour or two past when the whistle blows; it's just what we do to keep up with our ever increasing workloads. And with the prevalence of work from home, the lines between work and home life have become even more blurred.

When I ask people what time their workday ends, the answer is almost always something like, "Five o'clock, but I can't leave then. I usually wrap up around 6:30 or 7:00." Then when I ask if they could make it a point to end work on time, the reply is generally, "I can try, but I doubt it." When I press a little further on the issue, the reason for working late is usually that they feel they must or they're afraid they'll fall behind, not because their employer requires it.

To combat this, I suggest you start with a commitment to yourself to leave a little earlier each day. It's difficult for most at first, but it becomes easier over time, especially when you discover an extra hour of "me time" to water yourself.

If cutting back your work hours isn't feasible, there are plenty of other ways to make time for yourself. One of the best methods is to **schedule a standing appointment with yourself**. Put it on your calendar and KEEP IT.

Think about it this way.... When you have an important meeting with someone on your calendar, are you likely to cancel it if something of low or medium significance comes up, or are you going to hesitate because you don't want to send a message to the person that they aren't important? You're probably going to keep it unless the item that cropped up is quite serious and attending to it cannot be delayed. If that's the case for meetings with others, then why would you cancel on yourself?

YOU are your most important appointment, so it's time you start treating yourself like it. Show respect and love to your #1 (that's you!) by keeping the appointment with yourself.

If you find that life's daily priorities are getting in the way of your much needed and deserved "me time", then it's time to a look at and adjust your priorities.

Give it a try. Look at all the things you do on a daily and weekly basis to determine if they really must be done, or if they can be reprioritized so you can carve out some much needed "me time." Here is an exercise you can do to help you identify and structure your priorities:

1. Using the **Priority Checklist** provided at the end of this chapter, write down all the things you do or need to do on a regular basis. Things like going to work, walking the

dog, taking the kids to school, cooking dinner. Keep going until you've written everything down, no matter how big or small.

2. Check off the frequency with which these things need to get done – _not how often you currently do them_, but how often they _actually require being done_. Choose daily (D), weekly (W) or monthly (M).

3. Go through your list and categorize everything as one of the following:
    *   **Must Do** – These are the things that _must_ get done every day, week or month, like going to work, taking the kids to school, giving your dog flea control, etc.
    *   **Need to Do** – Need to do items differ from must do items because they don't necessarily _have_ to be done that day or right then, but _need_ to get done eventually. These are things like washing the dishes, doing laundry, making the bed, cleaning, and so on.
    *   **Nice to Do** – These are things you'd _like_ to do, whether they're fun or not, but you don't necessarily have the time. When you do have the time, they tend to come before your wants. These may be things like working out or organizing your closet.

Think carefully when categorizing things. Ask yourself questions like, "Is this something that _must_ get done or is it something that can wait an hour or a day or even a week?" The answer will differ for everyone. For some, washing the dishes immediately is a must, whereas for others, letting them sit for an hour or two (or even overnight) is okay.

4. After you've categorized everything, rank them according to their order of importance on a scale of one to five, with one (1) being most important and five (5) being least important. Again, think carefully about this and ask yourself, "How important is this *really* in the grand scheme of things?" If the item is something you want to do, but just can't seem to find the time for (working out is one I hear a lot), give it a higher priority.

Once you've created your list of priorities, defined how often they need to be done, and determined their level of importance, look for areas where you may have made some improvements or changes.

Were you able to take an activity that you were performing daily and change it to weekly? Is there something you thought of previously as a must do that has now become a need to do or nice to do? If so, use this newfound free time to engage in activities that you want to do but haven't been able to find the time for – **water yourself**.

If you didn't see a shift in priorities, take another look. Try to identify tasks that can be changed to allow more time for you. Look for new solutions to current obligations. For example, taking the kids to school or after-school activities – can they take the bus? Can you work out a carpool with a neighbor or friend to split responsibilities? (I'm sure that the other parent will be very grateful for the added free time when you handle carpool.)

Think in terms of new or different ways you can approach responsibilities that free up time for you. Even if it's only a little bit of time here and there, it all adds up!

You can find the **Priority Checklist** at the end of this chapter.

Watering Log

Date _____

How I watered myself _____
_____
_____
_____
_____

How I felt after watering _____
_____
_____
_____

Date _____

How I watered myself _____
_____
_____
_____

How I felt after watering _____
_____
_____
_____

Watering Log

Date _____

How I watered myself _____

_____

_____

_____

_____

How I felt after watering _____

_____

_____

_____

Date _____

How I watered myself _____

_____

_____

_____

_____

How I felt after watering _____

_____

_____

_____

Watering Log

Date _____

How I watered myself _____
_____
_____
_____
_____

How I felt after watering _____
_____
_____
_____

Date _____

How I watered myself _____
_____
_____
_____
_____

How I felt after watering _____
_____
_____
_____

Growth Tracker

Date _____

Pre-Watering

Before you begin watering yourself and tracking your progress, take stock of how you feel in this moment and jot your thoughts and feelings down on the lines below.

_____

_____

_____

_____

My Dreams

Write down 1 to 2 dreams you'd like to accomplish in your life and why these dreams are important to you.

Dream 1 _____

_____

Why this dream is important to me:

_____

_____

Dream 2 _____

_____

Why this dream is important to me:

_____

_____

Growth Tracker

Now it's time to start planning out the goals & milestones that will enable you to accomplish your dreams.

Goal 1_____

Date I want to accomplish this goal by: _____

How this goal gets me closer to my dreams:_____
_____

Milestones to achieve this goal...

Milestone	Due Date	How this helps me achieve my goal	Milestone Complete
			☐
			☐
			☐
			☐
			☐
			☐
			☐
			☐
			☐

Growth Tracker

Now it's time to start planning out the goals & milestones that will enable you to accomplish your dreams.

Goal 2 _____

Date I want to accomplish this goal by: _____

How this goal gets me closer to my dreams:_____

_____

Milestones to achieve this goal...

Milestone	Due Date	How this helps me achieve my goal	Milestone Complete
			☐
			☐
			☐
			☐
			☐
			☐
			☐
			☐
			☐

Growth Tracker

Now it's time to start planning out the goals & milestones that will enable you to accomplish your dreams.

Goal 3 _____

Date I want to accomplish this goal by: _____

How this goal gets me closer to my dreams: _____

_____

Milestones to achieve this goal...

Milestone	Due Date	How this helps me achieve my goal	Milestone Complete
			☐
			☐
			☐
			☐
			☐
			☐
			☐
			☐
			☐

Growth Tracker

As you work toward achieving your milestones, goals and dreams, it's important to regularly check in with yourself. Use this section to reflect on the progress you've made toward your goals and dreams, and how you're feeling.

End of Month 1   Date _____

Goals and/or Milestones I've accomplished:

_____

_____

_____

_____

How these accomplishments have brought me closer to my dreams:

_____

_____

_____

_____

How I'm feeling right now:

_____

_____

_____

_____

_____

Growth Tracker

End of Month 3   Date _____

Goals and/or Milestones I've accomplished:

_____

_____

_____

_____

How these accomplishments have brought me
closer to my dreams:

_____

_____

_____

_____

How I'm feeling right now:

_____

_____

_____

_____

_____

Notes:

_____

_____

_____

Growth Tracker

End of Month 6   **Date** _____

Goals and/or Milestones I've accomplished:

_____

_____

_____

_____

How these accomplishments have brought me
closer to my dreams:

_____

_____

_____

_____

How I'm feeling right now:

_____

_____

_____

_____

_____

Notes:

_____

_____

_____

Growth Tracker

End of Month 9   Date _____

Goals and/or Milestones I've accomplished:

_____

_____

_____

_____

How these accomplishments have brought me
closer to my dreams:

_____

_____

_____

_____

How I'm feeling right now:

_____

_____

_____

_____

_____

Notes:

_____

_____

_____

Growth Tracker

End of Month 12   Date _____

Goals and/or Milestones I've accomplished:

_____

_____

_____

_____

How these accomplishments have brought me
closer to my dreams:

_____

_____

_____

_____

How I'm feeling right now:

_____

_____

_____

_____

Notes:

_____

_____

_____

Priority Checklist

Find more "me time" by prioritizing the everyday tasks, chores and items that are taking up your time.

How to use this Checklist:

1. Write down the activity, item, task or chore.
2. Identify how often it needs to be done Daily (D), Weekly (W) or Monthly (M)
3. Prioritize the item as a Must Do (H), Need to Do (M), or Nice to Do (L).
4. Circle the level of importance of the Activity/Task with 1 being highest level of importance and 5 being lowest.

Once complete, look at how you prioritized your activities and tasks. If an item is an "H" and "1", then that's likely something you can't deprioritize. However, if an item is an "L", you should look at ways to remove that activity from your life or reduce the frequency with which you do it.

Once you identify the low priority, low importance items in your life, you should start see where you can free up time for your much needed "me time" to water yourself.

Priority Checklist

Activity/Task	Frequency	Priority	Importance
_____	D W M	H M L	1 2 3 4 5
_____	D W M	H M L	1 2 3 4 5
_____	D W M	H M L	1 2 3 4 5
_____	D W M	H M L	1 2 3 4 5
_____	D W M	H M L	1 2 3 4 5
_____	D W M	H M L	1 2 3 4 5
_____	D W M	H M L	1 2 3 4 5
_____	D W M	H M L	1 2 3 4 5
_____	D W M	H M L	1 2 3 4 5
_____	D W M	H M L	1 2 3 4 5
_____	D W M	H M L	1 2 3 4 5
_____	D W M	H M L	1 2 3 4 5
_____	D W M	H M L	1 2 3 4 5
_____	D W M	H M L	1 2 3 4 5
_____	D W M	H M L	1 2 3 4 5
_____	D W M	H M L	1 2 3 4 5

Frequency: D = Daily, W = Weekly, M = Monthly
Priority: H = Must Do, M = Need to Do, L = Nice to Do
Importance: 1 = High, 3 = Medium, 5 = Low

Priority Checklist

Activity/Task	Frequency	Priority	Importance
_____	D W M	H M L	1 2 3 4 5
_____	D W M	H M L	1 2 3 4 5
_____	D W M	H M L	1 2 3 4 5
_____	D W M	H M L	1 2 3 4 5
_____	D W M	H M L	1 2 3 4 5
_____	D W M	H M L	1 2 3 4 5
_____	D W M	H M L	1 2 3 4 5
_____	D W M	H M L	1 2 3 4 5
_____	D W M	H M L	1 2 3 4 5
_____	D W M	H M L	1 2 3 4 5
_____	D W M	H M L	1 2 3 4 5
_____	D W M	H M L	1 2 3 4 5
_____	D W M	H M L	1 2 3 4 5
_____	D W M	H M L	1 2 3 4 5
_____	D W M	H M L	1 2 3 4 5

Frequency: D = Daily, W = Weekly, M = Monthly
Priority: H = Must Do, M = Need to Do, L = Nice to Do
Importance: 1 = High, 3 = Medium, 5 = Low

Bask in the Sun

"We are shaped by our thoughts; we become
what we think. When the mind is pure,
joy follows like a shadow that never leaves."

Buddha

Sunlight is essential to a plant's growth. Without it, plants couldn't fuel the life-sustaining process they undergo to make their own food. Since I know you're dying to take a nostalgic trip down memory lane to elementary school science class, I'll refresh your memory on how that works.

Basically, a plant absorbs energy from the sun and then uses that energy to power a chemical process to convert carbon dioxide, absorbed through its leaves, and water, absorbed through its roots, into glucose and other basic carbohydrates. It then combines the glucose and carbohydrates with other minerals (also absorbed through its roots) to produce starch, fat and protein. These starches, fats and proteins are what fuel the plant's growth. As this fuel is burned off, the plant releases oxygen through its leaves into the atmosphere, providing us with one of our most basic needs for survival.

The amount of sunlight a plant needs depends on several factors, including the plant species and habitat. Some plants require direct sunlight, while others need only partial light. Several plants can even thrive with negligible light. But one thing is certain – almost all plants require some level of sunlight to grow and live. It's essential.

Now that I've gone all science geek, you may be asking, "What does all of this botany talk have to do with me?" There's the obvious symbiotic relationship of plants cleansing our air of the carbon dioxide we expel and converting it into the oxygen we breathe to sustain life.

Beyond that, we also need sunlight – no, *sunshine* – to fuel us and help us grow.

What's the difference? **Sunlight** comes from the sun. It's a quantifiable element (think UV indexes and "partially sunny" days). But **sunshine**, that's what makes us feel good both inside and out. It evokes feelings of joy and contentment, conjures lighthearted thoughts of skipping through meadows, induces the peaceful sound of waves crashing on the shoreline, and summons the loving feeling of a warm embrace.

The Power of Words

As humans, we have basic biological and physiological needs – air, food, water, shelter, sleep. We also have another set of needs that help us to walk in our purpose and achieve self-actualization. These needs include affection, relationships, personal growth and fulfillment.[8] For the most part, we are able to take care of our basic needs, but fulfilling the needs required to live a purposeful life and achieve self-actualization require more attention, and sunshine plays an important role in helping us attain these things.

In the previous chapter I talked about water, and I want to discuss it a bit further here as it has a lot to do with sunshine. The human body is made up of approximately 70 percent water – without it, we would not exist. We all know that we must maintain proper hydration to stay healthy, but did you know that the balance and state of the water in your body could also affect your happiness and wellbeing?

Dr. Masaru Emoto was a Doctor of Alternative Medicine who studied the effects of thoughts, words and feelings on water. Through his studies, he found that the energy expelled through words, thoughts and feelings has a profound effect on the way water crystals form when frozen.[3,4]

Dr. Emoto conducted a series of experiments, taking water and exposing it to words that were both positive and negative in nature. He did this using both written and spoken words and phrases, and observed remarkable results. The water that was exposed to positive words and phrases produced beautiful, well-formed crystals. On the other hand, the water that was exposed to negative words and phrases yielded crystals that were deformed and broken. These results were the same whether he used purified water or impure water, demonstrating that regardless of the water's initial state or source, positivity led to a beautiful outcome.[3,4]

In his book, The Hidden Messages in Water, Dr. Emoto talks about his experiments and draws the conclusion that since our bodies are made up of 70 percent water, we can infer that the way in which we talk to and think about ourselves affects the water within our body and, therefore, has a direct effect on our overall health and wellbeing. The same can be said for the way we let others speak to and treat us.[4]

Dr. Emoto conducted a similar experiment on rice with an analogous outcome. He put rice into three glass beakers and covered the rice with water. He then said, "Thank you" to one, "You're an idiot" to another and completely ignored the third every day for one month. The rice that had been thanked fermented and turned a beautiful golden color, the rice that had been told, "You're an idiot" turned black, and the rice that had been ignored began to rot. This experiment demonstrates further the impact that thoughts and words have on physical states.[7]

I know it may sound incredulous that words taped on or spoken to a glass jar filled with water or rice could affect the very makeup of what is contained within. I find it quite remarkable myself, and many people have attempted to replicate and debunk Dr. Emoto's experiments, with mixed results. But one thing is certain – after practicing positive thought and talk in my own life, and watching others integrate it into theirs, I can personally attest to the transformative power of positivity.

Whether you believe Dr. Emoto's findings or not, there are numerous studies that all point to the same outcome – positivity leads to increased happiness and personal fulfillment. Believing in yourself and surrounding yourself with others who believe in and support you can lead you to new heights you once only imagined.

Numerous experts in the field of psychology have conducted tests on the effects of positivity and negativity on our personal and business relationships, happiness, satisfaction and wellbeing. The outcomes of those studies provide compelling evidence that positive thoughts and words lead to a happier and healthier life. Alternatively, negative thoughts and words lead to increased anxiety, depression and negative feelings.

According to an article published in *Psychology Today* by Dr. Andrew Newberg and Mark Waldman, "just seeing a list of negative words for a few seconds will make a highly anxious or depressed person feel worse, and the more you ruminate on them, the more you can actually damage key structures that regulate your memory, feelings, and emotions."[11]

Conversely, research show that positive thoughts can enhance your sense of happiness, increase your life satisfaction and improve your overall wellbeing, even if those positive thoughts are irrational.[11] That just goes to show the power of positive thinking - you can drastically improve your outlook on life just by changing your way of thinking!

Get Your Daily Dose
This brings me back to sunshine. I'm not talking about sunshine in the traditional sense of getting outside and absorbing some vitamin D (which is also important to our overall health and happiness); I'm talking about a very different form of sunshine – positivity – and we can get it in a number of ways. Sunshine can come into your life through family and friends, your job/career, spiritual practice and meditation, hobbies, and doing nice deeds for others, among other things.

Positive words, phrases and thoughts are some of the most powerful forms of sunshine you can receive. What you tell yourself and allow others to tell you deeply shapes your being, and continuous exposure to positive reinforcement can be extremely impactful.

Everyone's sources of sunshine are different, but there's one source of sunshine that's important for everyone – the sunshine that comes from within. **How you perceive yourself and what you tell yourself shape not only who you are, but also who you become.**

Seems pretty simple – change your thinking, change your life. But did you know that it takes a minimum of three, and a recommended five, positive thoughts to counteract the effect of *just one* negative thought?[11] If you're shocked and worried by that stat, don't be! It may sound like a lot of work to overcome the negative with positive; but with time and practice it becomes your way of thinking and being, ultimately bringing more sunshine into your life, and making you much happier and healthier.

How many times have you looked in the mirror and frowned at the person staring back at you? How many times have you told yourself "I'm fat," "I'm not good enough," "There's no way I could do that."? Why is it that we tend to focus on the negative and pick ourselves apart when we have so much to offer the world?

Did you know that telling yourself that you can't do something – or worse, speaking it out loud and frowning while you say it – releases stress chemicals in your brain and affects decision-making centers in your frontal lobe that lead to irrational thoughts and actions?[10] This means that the more you tell yourself that you are fat, ugly and stupid, the more you'll believe it. And negative words and phrases have a much deeper and more permanent effect on you than positive ones. The reason for this is that our brains are naturally hard-wired to quickly react to things that threaten our survival or wellbeing, and negative words do just that.[10]

The practice of cognitive therapy has recognized this for decades. Psychologist Aaron T. Beck, a pioneer in cognitive psychology, established three principles of cognitive therapy. One of these principles states that our emotions are created by our thoughts, which means how we feel is directly related to what we're thinking about. His other two principles go on to state that "depression is the constant thinking of negative thoughts" and that most of our negative thoughts are either "just plain wrong or distortions of the truth" that we accept without question.[1]

That's why it is critically important to transform your thinking. By focusing on the positive elements in your life and telling yourself that you are smart, beautiful and capable, you begin to embrace that truth. I'm sure you've heard the old saying, "perception is reality." Well, it's true. How you perceive people and experiences is how they will manifest as truths in your mind, and those truths will paint your feelings and emotions.

If you perceive a situation as bad or think that everyone is out to get you - true or not - that is what you will believe. However, if you stop to process the situation, alter your perspective and start looking at the world in a new light, you may begin to realize that some of the bad or stressful things going on around you have nothing to do with you, or that they simply aren't as bad as you may have once thought.

That's not to say that we don't have negative experiences, thoughts or feelings, we absolutely do; they are a part of life, and it is important to both acknowledge and process them. What I'm suggesting is that it is important to pay attention to your thoughts and feelings and what is driving them. Are you thinking or feeling a certain way based on past experiences, or because it is the right thought or feeling for the situation at hand? **Mindfulness is the first step to transforming your thoughts, feelings and outlook on life.** Only once you've become mindful of why you're thinking and feeling the way you are, can you begin to retrain your brain for positivity.

Transforming your way of thinking is no easy task, especially when it comes to outside factors. That's why I recommend starting with something you can actually control – yourself. Once you start to see yourself in a new light, you can then focus outwardly and begin to look at situations and other people differently.

As I write this, I can't help but be reminded of the 2006 movie Ladybugs starring Rodney Dangerfield. In the beginning of the movie, Rodney Dangerfield's character is attending a seminar where the speaker has the participants look in a mirror and recite out loud, "I am great! I am wonderful! Everybody likes me!"

It may seem silly, but looking in the mirror and speaking positive affirmations out loud can go a long way in helping to boost your confidence and change your self-perception. In fact, did you know that **your brain fires up to 10,000 more neurons when you *speak* out loud versus only 100 neurons** when you only think about something?[10] That's pretty powerful stuff. **Just by saying something out loud, your brain is 100 times more likely to listen!**

So throw caution to the wind. Shout from the rooftop, "I am great! I am wonderful! Everybody likes me!" Or maybe something like, "I am smart! I am beautiful! I can conquer anything!"

Customize it – what do you need to hear? Go ahead, put the book down and head over to a mirror right now to try it. I can wait.

I believe in you

you look great ♡

It's A good day

Congratulations! You just used sunshine to fuel yourself similarly to how plants use sunlight to fuel their own growth. Practice this regularly. Look in the mirror and tell yourself 3 to 5 positive affirmations every day. When you're not in a place to shout it out, say it in your head (as we now know, saying it out loud is much more powerful...but something is always better than nothing). Whatever the circumstance, feed yourself positive thoughts. Continued exposure to sunshine will provide you with a steady fuel source that will nourish your health and happiness.

A Healthy Dose
So how much sunshine is enough? That really depends on you. Earlier in the chapter, I discussed how different types of plants require different amounts of sunlight – full, partial, low. We're similar to plants in that we also need different levels of sunshine.

According to happiness experts, 50% of our happiness level is controlled by our genetics, 10% is related to our circumstances, and the remaining 40% is thought to come from intentional activity.[12] What does this tell us?

Some people are naturally more positive than others. If you're one of these people, a.k.a. an eternal optimist or glass-half-full kind of person, then you're one of the lucky ones. Although you still need sunshine regularly, you may not need as much as someone who tends to see the glass half empty.

If you find yourself struggling to focus on the positive in your life, you're going to need a higher dose of sunshine to be able to grow and bloom. Because it's in your nature to focus on the negative things that happen in your life, you'll need to exert a little extra effort to ensure you get more sunshine from both yourself and others.

The 40% of happiness that is controlled by intentional activity is where sunshine comes in. By being intentional in *how* you spend your time, *who* you spend it with, your *thoughts* and *feelings*, you can significantly increase your overall happiness. Now that's something to be happy about!

Carpe Solem

It's never too late to seize the sunshine in your life. Regardless of where you've been in life or where you currently are, you can change where you're going. Each and every one of us starts out in a different station in life. We don't choose how we're born, who we're born to or where we're born. Likewise, we have limited control over our childhood upbringing. Some of us experience hard knocks and tragedy, while others are afforded all the love and opportunity the world has to offer. These experiences shape us and our perceptions about others, our future and ourselves; but they don't have to define our path in life. You **can** change your future. I'm not saying it will be easy, but it is possible.

Think back to the water crystals in Dr. Emoto's experiments. One of the interesting findings from the experiments was that regardless of the source of the water – pure mineral water or ordinary tap water – positive and negative words had the *same effect on both*. When exposed to positive words and phrases, both pure and impure water morphed into beautiful, well-formed crystals. And when exposed to negative words and phrases, both formed fragmented, distorted crystals.

The moral of the story? The power that positive and negative thoughts and words have on you is tremendous. Regardless of where you came from, what you've done or who you've been, you *can* alter the trajectory of your life. You hold the key to happiness and can grow and flourish in this life —increasing your sunshine will help you get where you want to be.

Ways to Catch Some Rays

We all need a little more sunshine in our lives. Here are some ways you can get some much-needed rays.

Mirror, mirror

Do people tell you you're beautiful, smart or talented, but you don't believe it or discount it? People are three times more likely to hand out a negative comment than a compliment, so chances are they mean it. And it's time you start embracing it as well.

You are your number one source of sunshine. Look in the mirror and tell yourself at least three (3) positive things every day. Why three? Because, as mentioned earlier in the chapter, it takes at least three, and as many as five, positive words or phrases to offset just one negative one. Can't think of three? That's okay! Start with one and gradually work yourself up to more, with the goal being at least five every day.

By changing your perceptions, you can help shape your reality. So stand tall in front of the mirror and tell yourself every day how great you are and believe it. You'll be surprised what it does for your self-confidence and outlook.

Open the blinds and let some light in

Sunshine comes from all different places. While it's crucial for you to find your internal source of sunshine, it's also important to get sunshine from external sources. The following five questions will help you identify some of your external sources of sunshine.

I recommend going through these questions multiple times. The first time you answer the questions, write down the answers that come to you quickly; don't give them too much thought. Then, go through the questions again later, taking time to invest thought into each answer. This could be later the same day, the next day or even a week later – the key is to take your time to think about it, then come back to it when you're ready.

1. **When** do you feel happiest?
2. **Where** do you feel happiest?
3. What **activities** make you feel happy?
4. **Who** brings joy to your life?
5. What is your **favorite** part of the day/favorite thing to do each day?

You'll want to revisit these questions as you see fit until you really start to get a handle on where your sunshine is coming from.

Now that you have identified some of your sources of sunshine, it's time to make sure you're getting regular exposure. Don't wait until you've had the opportunity to get this exactly right; start immediately after you answer the questions the first time by incorporating one thing that brings you sunshine into every day. Once that becomes part of your daily routine, add another and then another. Surround yourself with people who, and participate in activities that, bring you sunshine.

If you find that you're struggling to answer these questions, that's okay. Sometimes it's not always easy to identify your sources of sunshine, especially when you've been hiding out in the shade or your garden is full of weeds, pests and parasites (we'll get to that). If you're unable to answer these questions right now, set this exercise aside, start working on your Sunshine Journal, and come back to it later.

Keep a Sunshine Journal
Take note of things that make you happy and record them in a dedicated Sunshine Journal. Write down any and everything that makes you feel good. These can be small things that make you chuckle, people who make you smile, a pet, compliments, looking in the mirror and feeling good about yourself, being recognized for doing something well at work, and other positive experiences. Write it all down, no matter how big or small (every little bit of sunshine counts). Visit your journal regularly and look for patterns of things that make you feel good, happy, joyous or proud (in a good way). Then incorporate more of these activities and people into your life.

For example, if there's a co-worker you go to when you're having a bad day at work, and they always seem to make you smile without fail, that's a person that brings you sunshine. Or if every time you walk through the door and are greeted by your dog with his tail wagging, and you can't help but feel warm and smooshy inside (you know what I'm talking about), your furry friend is a source of sunshine.

Use your **Sunshine Journal** not only as a way to identify sources of sunshine in your life, but also as a source of sunshine itself. If you're feeling down, overwhelmed or stressed out, turn to your **Sunshine Journal**. Reading about the good people and experiences in your life can help alleviate stress, anxiety and sadness by reminding you of all the positive you have in your life. I've provided a handful of pages at the end of this chapter, complete with positive quotes, to get you started on your **Sunshine Journal**.

Help Others
Studies have shown that people who regularly help others tend to be happier and healthier than people who don't. This may seem cumbersome in your busy life filled with obligations and errands, so start small. Don't try to take on the world by committing to a big volunteer job if you don't have the time (if you do, then great, go for it!).

Try doing one thing for one person each day, no matter how small. It could be picking up copies from the copier and delivering them to a co-worker, cooking dinner for your spouse when you know they had a long day or holding the elevator door for someone instead of hitting the "close" button. You may not realize it, but random acts of kindness, no matter how small, have a positive effect on not only the people you're helping, but also yourself.

Robert Putnam, bestselling author of *Bowling Alone*, shares some compelling evidence to support this. He states that regular club attendance, volunteering, entertaining or church attendance is the happiness equivalent of more than **doubling** your income, and that civic connections have the happiness equivalent of **quadrupling** your income! Best of all, it doesn't take much work to reap the incredible rewards of helping others and getting involved in your community – you only need to volunteer, entertain or go to club meetings approximately once a month to get BIG happiness returns. As if that's not enough, here's a bonus...if you belong to no groups but decide to join *just one*, you cut your risk of dying over the next year in **half!**[13]

There's enough sunshine for everyone, so share it! In the great words of Buddha, "Thousands of candles can be lighted from a single candle, and the life of the candle will not be shortened. Happiness never decreases by being shared."

Sunshine Journal

"Know what sparks the light in you.
Then use that light to illuminate the world."
~Oprah Winfrey

_____
_____
_____
_____
_____
_____
_____
_____
_____
_____
_____
_____
_____
_____
_____
_____
_____
_____
_____
_____
_____
_____

Sunshine Journal

"Whoever is happy will make others happy too."
~Anne Frank

Sunshine Journal

"Say something positive, and you'll see something positive."
~Jim Thompson

Sunshine Journal

"Do good and good will come to you."
~Adam Lowy

Sunshine Journal

"Everything you can imagine is real."
~Pablo Picasso

Weed Your Garden

"What lies behind you and what lies in front of you,
pales in comparison to what lies inside of you."

Ralph Waldo Emerson

Now that you've taken a step outside and begun to let the sunshine in, it's time to start pulling some weeds to make room for growth. In a garden, yard or other venue, weeds are plants that generally have no value. They don't contribute to the garden in any way; in fact, they rob the garden and its plants of essential nutrients, water and sunlight needed to grow and bloom. This leaves the plants weak and prone to disease and infestation. In some cases, if weeds are left to grow out of control, they can be extremely invasive and, before you know it, overtake the garden.

Weeds tend to creep into our lives as well, some being more noticeable than others. Weeds are tasks, activities and chores that are unwelcome or cause undue stress and tension in our lives. Things in your life that could be considered a weed include your job, daunting tasks, chores, overwhelming activities and health issues.

Some weeds we can control; others we cannot or may have limited control over. For example, we can't control our DNA, which predisposes us to certain medical conditions. And it's quite difficult for us to control things such as our workload at the office or having to pick up our kids from soccer practice. But we can control many things in our life, especially the activities we engage in and how frequently we need to do mundane chores.

Identifying Weeds
The first step to removing weeds from your life is to identify them. Some weeds will be easy to spot, while others may be

difficult to detect. How do you identify weeds in your life? Just like weeds in a garden strangle a plant's growth and adversely affect its ability to blossom, weeds in your life do the same. Ask yourself what in your life is robbing you of your much needed "me time," health, happiness and overall wellbeing. **Awareness** is the key to identifying weeds. Being tuned in to how your life is affected by the activities you engage in and things that surround you is vital to recognizing a weed.

Pay attention to how certain activities in your life make you feel. If you look forward to doing something and feel excited, uplifted or rejuvenated after doing it, it could be a source of sunshine. However, if you dread going somewhere or doing something, and feel utterly exhausted, overwhelmed or discontented once you leave a place or finish an activity, it could be a weed. For example, do you dread going to PTA meetings? Do they leave you feeling drained, or do you find them just plain boring? If so, maybe you should resign from the PTA – it's not for everyone.

When thinking about weeds, be sure to carefully consider things that damage your health, alter your state of mind, or leave you feeling guilty or ashamed - either while you're in the act of doing it or later on. Are you drowning your sorrows in alcohol? Binge-eating away a bad day? Sleeping with people in hopes that they'll like you? While these things may make you feel good in the moment, the alleviation is temporary and most people end up feeling ashamed, guilty or worse after the fact, whether they admit it or not. In addition, these behaviors can become cyclical and destructive to your mind, body and spirit.

The key to ending these behaviors is to identify the root cause behind the behavior. For example, I happen to be an idle eater; I get the urge to mindlessly eat for no reason. It took me a while to figure this out. I'd find myself in the kitchen, shoving my face full of food – a bite here, a bite there – but I wasn't even hungry. I finally started asking myself, "Why are you eating?" and began looking for a pattern as to why I was eating if I wasn't hungry. That's when I realized, if I sat in one place for too long, I wanted to eat. It was a way to keep my overactive-self busy.

Once I figured out why I was eating, I was able to come up with a solution to help control it. First, I stopped keeping a stockpile of snacks readily available, especially unhealthy ones. This helped for the times I found myself wandering around the kitchen, opening the fridge and pantry doors looking for something to munch on. If I didn't find something I could easily shove in my mouth, and I wasn't hungry enough to make something, I would go back to what I was doing without the unnecessary snack.

Second, I learned to keep myself busy. I know I'm not a person that can sit for hours on end, even if I'm doing work. To combat this, I make sure to break up my day with meetings or get up from my desk to stretch or go for a walk. Even a quick trip to the bathroom helps me to break up the monotony.

The key to getting rid of a bad behavior or issue in your life is to identify why it's occurring, then work on fixing the underlying cause. If you're a binge-eater, figure out why you're binge eating. Look for patterns in your behavior or activities that occur on the days you binge eat to identify why you're doing it and determine if those things can be changed or eliminated.

If it's your job, what is it about your job that distresses you? If it doesn't happen every day, what is occurring on the days when you do feel upset? Maybe it's a specific task or person you interact with. Be cognizant of what's happening on the days you feel stressed or angry. Once you've pinpointed what the true issue is, look for ways to eliminate it or change the circumstances surrounding that weed.

In addition, figure out a method that helps you to control the unwanted behavior. Let's stick with binge eating for now. If you've had a particularly rough day and are feeling like you want to go home and soothe yourself with food, instead of going straight home, stop at the gym and exercise (keep a packed gym bag in the car so you don't have any excuses). If that's not feasible, try meditating to calm yourself or go for a walk to clear your head. Then, if you still want to eat, ask yourself, "Why am I eating? Am I hungry? Am I stressed? Do I need to eat?"

Weeding Techniques
When dealing with weeds, you can either pull them or redirect their growth. Before pulling a weed, think about the tradeoff you need to make to remove it from your life and what its removal will mean to your overall wellbeing. For the weeds in your life that can't be pulled, you can reduce their burden by redirecting their growth. In these situations, think about how you can approach dealing with that weed differently than you currently do.

For example, if you absolutely hate cleaning the house, look into getting a cleaning service (pull the weed). Or if you feel like you're constantly taking on all the chores in the house, create a chore chart to share the burden with your family or roommates (redirect its growth).

I used to feel as if there was no way to remove daunting things from my life and made all kinds of excuses as to why they just had to stay there and torture me. Let's continue to use cleaning as an example. I'm pretty good about cleaning up after myself on a daily basis so that mess doesn't accumulate or become overwhelming, but there's always the task of deeper cleaning. You have to mop the floors, scrub the toilet and shower, dust...never things I enjoyed doing, especially after a long, hard week at work. All I wanted to do was sit back, kick my feet up, wiggle my nose, say "abracadabra," and the cleaning would be done. But real life doesn't work that way. So I made a tradeoff that yielded a solution.

My roommate at the time was feeling the same stress I was, so he suggested that we split the cost to have a cleaning service come in. We were both busy professionals who had very little free time on our hands, so why should we waste it on cleaning? He made a good case, but I wasn't sure if I wanted to spend my hard-earned money on a cleaning service. When I did the cost-benefit analysis – a little bit of money out of my pocket each month in exchange for hours of freedom and one less burden on my already overflowing plate – I bit the bullet and agreed. Let me tell you, pulling that one little weed made my life exponentially better and allowed me to focus on more important and fulfilling things.

I no longer needed to spend my precious and limited time on weekends scrubbing and mopping. I could use that time I got back to water myself.

Since pulling this weed came with a financial obligation, it also came with a tradeoff. I had to be willing to give up something else in exchange, so I decided I would skip a dinner out and make a home-cooked meal instead (which provided additional health benefits in the long run). Thirteen years, a move and a marriage later, I'm **still** using a cleaning service. That's a weed I never want back in my life.

If pulling one of your weeds requires a financial obligation, think about what tradeoff you can make. Maybe it's making coffee at home instead of hitting up the local coffee shop daily, or packing your lunch instead of going out to eat every day – you get the idea. The bottom line is to look at your weeds and ask yourself, "Can this weed be pulled? If so, what is the tradeoff?" If the tradeoff is worth it, then take steps to make it happen. And if there's no downside or tradeoff to getting rid of a pesky weed, that's a big win!

If the weed can't be pulled, look at ways in which you can redirect its growth. Do you dread coming home and cooking dinner every night after a busy day at work? Try making food for the week when you have a day off and a little extra time. You don't have to make the same thing for every day – cook a variety of dishes, store them in the fridge or freezer, and pull them out when you need them. Make a couple of different main dishes and a few different sides so you won't get bored. When you get home after a long day, pull out what you want to eat, heat it up and enjoy not only the meal, but also the extra time. Then relax, kick your feet up, and enjoy doing whatever it is that makes you happy. If cooking isn't your thing, try a prepared meal service or order delivery.

It all comes back to perspective. Change your way of thinking and your approach to things, and you will change your life. This will help you to weed out or redirect the things in life that burden you, allowing more time for watering and sunshine. Does this mean you can get rid of every single weed in your life? Not necessarily, but you can significantly reduce them, along with the stress and unhappiness they cause.

Weeds come in all shapes and sizes. We've talked about some of the smaller ones, but there are much bigger ones, such as your job, that may not be so easy to tackle. These weeds can be very complex and difficult to deal with, so much so that they become intertwined with you, making their removal damaging or even impossible. In these cases, you need to redirect the weed or cut it back to allow more sunshine in and make room for your personal growth. When removal of a difficult weed *is* possible, it may be a long process that requires a little bit of patience and careful gardening on your part.

According to the 2022 State of the Global Workplace Gallup Report, a mere "21% of employees are engaged at work" and only "33% of employees are thriving in their overall wellbeing." The report further states that, "most would say that they don't find their work meaningful, don't think their lives are going well or don't feel hopeful about their future."[15]

Those are some pretty bleak stats; and if this sounds like you, your job is likely a weed.

So what happens if you continue to stay in a job or career that makes you miserable? One that you wake up every morning and force yourself to go to, but dread; and then when you get there, you spend eight-plus hours doing. Have you thought about how the increased and persistent stress is affecting your health and happiness? Bear with me while I go a little science geek on you again.

When you're placed in a stressful situation, your brain responds by preparing your body to defend itself. This causes the nervous system to go into "fight or flight" mode, kicking into overdrive and releasing hormones that sharpen your senses, tense your muscles, quicken your pulse and deepen your breathing. This is an important built-in defense mechanism that your body undergoes, and it's critical in life-threatening situations because it helps us survive. The problem is, the human body wasn't built to be in this state for extended periods of time, and when it is, systems become fatigued and damage can ensue.

This means that placing yourself in situations that lead to a state of ongoing stress wears down your body and immune system, leading to an increased chance of illness or injury. And in many cases, our jobs and finances are large contributing factors to our stress levels.

Don't get me wrong. I'm not telling you to just up and quit your job if you're stressed or unhappy in your current career. There are bills to pay and mouths to feed. What I am saying is to assess how much that job affects your overall wellbeing. If it's weighing on you and adversely affecting your mental, emotional or physical health, look at ways in which you can improve your current work situation. If you don't feel improvement is possible, or you've exhausted all available options, it may be time to consider a change. Easier said than done, right?

Weeding From Experience

After more than a decade in a successful sales and marketing career where I only saw myself climbing higher, I decided I needed a change. I was good at my job and even enjoyed it most of the time, but at the end of the day I found it unfulfilling and extremely stressful. I wasn't walking in my purpose − to help people − and it was taking a toll on me.

I decided to do something about this weed, so I went back to school (while still working) and obtained a certification in holistic health coaching. After I was fully certified and able to start seeing clients, I dove in headfirst and started making client appointments at night and on the weekends.

As I started to see positive change in the lives of the people I was helping, /felt empowered and happy, and began to feel less and less content with my full-time career. I longed to leave the corporate environment so that I could make helping people through coaching my full-time career. But I was terrified of going from an executive level position where I was making six figures and living comfortably, to having negative income as I started and built my own business. So I came up with a foolproof plan (or so I thought).... Build up my clientele to a profitable point, then quit my job. Boy, was I in for a rude awakening.

My plan wasn't as easy as I had imagined. The workload at my day job kept getting heavier and heavier, taking away from my ability to have time (and energy) to write a business plan and complete the tasks necessary to get a business off the ground. In addition, I felt that if I couldn't fully devote myself to my clients' needs, I shouldn't be working with them (I just didn't see it as fair). So I scaled back my clientele to a more manageable number, which got me absolutely nowhere in making a full-time career change.

At the same time, I was inspired to write this book. It has been my dream since I was a kid to write a book, and I felt passionate about turning it into a reality. In addition, I saw this book as my opportunity to really help people on a larger scale, something that has always been a personal motivator. So I said to myself, cut back on clients, write the book, sell the book, then quit your job! Again, not nearly as easy as it sounded in my head – not that it wasn't possible, it was, but with all the other extracurricular activities on my plate, not to mention planning my wedding at the same time, I was overextending myself again.

Still I wrote; and as I wrote, something remarkable happened. Here I was, writing a book about watering yourself, getting more sunshine and removing weeds from your life, yet I wasn't taking my own advice. I needed to pull a weed, plant a new seed, and water the heck out of it! So I did.

After months of conversations with my then-fiancé (now husband), I developed a plan that would allow me to chase my dreams and pull that big ole job weed. I love teaching and had always wanted to teach at the college level, so I applied for teaching jobs and then left my executive sales and marketing career to become a part-time adjunct instructor teaching public speaking and communications courses. This helped me in multiple ways: 1) it provided me with income so I wasn't just diving off the deep end without a parachute (although teachers, even college instructors, are severely underpaid – a discussion for another day). 2) It allowed me to live my dream of teaching and inspiring the next generation. 3) Because it was part-time, I had the freedom and flexibility to dig in and finish my book before turning my focus to building a coaching practice.

I'll never forget the response from the President of the company where I was working when I resigned. He asked me why I was leaving, and I told him it was to write a book. He looked astounded and told me that was "a first." He was baffled that I didn't have another full-time job lined up, but he congratulated me and said to let him know when my book came out and he'd be sure to buy it. After giving me his best wishes and thanking me for my service, we said our goodbyes and I walked down the hall.

As I was walking away, I heard him come out of his office and say to his executive assistant with astonishment in his voice, "Did Shannon tell you why she's leaving? She's writing a book." I chuckled to myself, because I knew it sounded crazy – leave the safety and security of a great job where I was making good money to write a book and pray it sells, then start a business from scratch. Ha! That did sound insane. But I also felt better than I ever had in my life. The result? You're holding it in your hand.

I won't say it's been an easy road. It certainly hasn't. Building a business is expensive, and writing a book is a time-consuming process that doesn't reap financial rewards unless it sells. At the time that I originally wrote this book, I was making negative income, putting more money into getting my business started than I was getting back, digging into my savings account and having to be more frugal than ever before. I was also working harder than I ever had.

Now, I have a successful public speaking, communication and confidence coaching practice and a technology startup (I just can't seem to get enough of starting new things – innovation fuels me). Although it's been a long, hard and windy journey to discovering my purpose and aligning it with work that fulfills me, I wouldn't change a thing. I'm happier now after stepping out on faith because I get to help people every day while chasing my dreams. That brings me joy and happiness – something you can't place a value on.

Why do I share this with you? To let you know that weeds big and small can be pulled. You just have to have faith in yourself and blaze a path to your dreams. With proper planning and the right approach, you *can* remove or redirect the growth of a weed, leaving a lot more room for water and sunshine in your life.

Growing Conditions

Weeds thrive when favorable growing conditions are present. If you don't address the weed, it will persist, and may even grow larger. Let's continue to use the job example. If your workload at the office is looming over you like a piano hanging from a frayed rope on the verge of snapping, speak with your boss. I know this may sound scary, but in my experience as both an employee and leader, I've found that this is generally effective. Any time I've spoken to my boss about my heavy workload or issues I was experiencing, they listened and tried to make whatever change was in their power. Of course, there were times when my boss told me there was nothing they could do in the current moment and asked me to hang in there, but they always let me know my voice was heard and tried to make some kind of change or provide relief as soon as possible, even when I was told initially "it is what it is."

As a manager, it was always my goal to help my employees enjoy what they were doing, and many bosses feel the same way. Happy employees are productive employees. When you are unhappy in your job, you become unproductive, discontented and, eventually, detrimental to the workplace – something nobody wants. If you don't speak up and let your boss know you're overwhelmed or unhappy, they may never know, and the work will keep coming, causing you to become more overloaded and unhappy. In essence, you're creating favorable conditions to allow that weed to continue to grow and negatively affect you.

To determine if you're creating favorable growing conditions for weeds, start by asking yourself the following questions:

1. What do I have control over?
2. Am I enabling or allowing this situation to occur or continue?
3. Is there something I can do to stop this from happening or change the situation?

Introspection is the first step in the removal and prevention of weeds. Look at what actions you're taking that may be allowing the growth of weeds in your life. If you stop providing favorable conditions for weed growth, the abundance of weeds in your life will decrease significantly.

The next step is to determine the proper action to take. Once you've concluded whether or not you have control over the weed's presence, you can then decide how you can either rid your life of whatever it is (pull the weed) or find a way to lessen the impact it has on your life (redirect its growth).

A fair word of warning, though – weeds are persistent. You may have to deal with them multiple times in order to rid your life of them, and you can expect new weeds to crop up. No matter how good your efforts are to prevent weeds in your life, you can bet that some of them will find their way in. Managing weeds is an ongoing process if you want to flourish and grow to your maximum potential, but it *is* possible and it all starts with you.

Reap What You Sow

Here are some simple ways you can identify and deal with weeds in your life.

Document weeds
Use the **Weeds Checklist** at the end of this chapter to create a list of all the things in your life that bring you unhappiness, stress or pain. Then, keep the list in a handy place so that you can add to it as other weeds crop up. Weeds can include:

- Small annoyances
- Daunting everyday tasks or chores
- Things that make you feel guilty, bad, sad or that you just plain hate doing
- Stressors

Identify which weeds will be easiest to remove from your life and start with those. If it's walking the dog, try installing a doggy door so your dog can go out on her own. If it's cooking dinner every night, try making enough food for the week on the weekends, then portion it out and set it aside for grab-and-go dinners. If it's taking the kids to soccer practice, work with another parent to set up a carpool where you split responsibilities (they'll probably be thankful too). The key is to think about how you can either remove this thing from your life or reduce the burden of it.

Then, as you begin to pull weeds or redirect their growth, check them off your list. Work through your weeds one at a time until you have them all checked off. If you can't check them all off (some weeds may be inevitable), focus on keeping the persistent weeds under control so they don't take over your life. As your life becomes less inhabited by weeds, you'll start to feel lighter, happier and freer.

Keep a Weeds Journal
Similar to the Sunshine Journal, start a **Weeds Journal** in which you only write negative thoughts, feelings and experiences. This journal will help you to identify additional weeds that you may not have realized were present. You can then add them to your Weeds Checklist and start the removal or redirection process.

Why keep a separate **Weeds Journal**?

1. Having a journal dedicated to weeds will help you to more easily identify things that are creating undue stress and roadblocks to your happiness and fulfillment. Add recurring things from your journal to your Weeds Checklist so you can then work to remove or mitigate the effects of those things.
2. Keeping a Weeds Journal separate from your Sunshine Journal will prevent the negative from overflowing into the positive, thus allowing you to more easily see all of the good you have in your life.

At the end of this chapter, I've provided some **Weeds Journal** pages to get you started.

Weeds Checklist

Weed	Removed	Redirected
_____	☐	☐
_____	☐	☐
_____	☐	☐
_____	☐	☐
_____	☐	☐
_____	☐	☐
_____	☐	☐
_____	☐	☐
_____	☐	☐
_____	☐	☐
_____	☐	☐
_____	☐	☐
_____	☐	☐
_____	☐	☐
_____	☐	☐
_____	☐	☐

Weeds Checklist

Weed	Removed	Redirected
_____	☐	☐
_____	☐	☐
_____	☐	☐
_____	☐	☐
_____	☐	☐
_____	☐	☐
_____	☐	☐
_____	☐	☐
_____	☐	☐
_____	☐	☐
_____	☐	☐
_____	☐	☐
_____	☐	☐
_____	☐	☐
_____	☐	☐
_____	☐	☐

Weeds Journal

"The struggle you're in today is developing
the strength you need tomorrow."
~Robert Tew

_____

_____

_____

_____

_____

_____

_____

_____

_____

_____

_____

_____

_____

_____

_____

_____

_____

_____

_____

_____

Weeds Journal

"Never fear shadows. They simply mean
there's a light shining nearby."
~Ruth E. Renkel

Weeds Journal

"Nothing is impossible.
The word itself says, "I'm possible!""
~Audrey Hepburn

_____
_____
_____
_____
_____
_____
_____
_____
_____
_____
_____
_____
_____
_____
_____
_____
_____
_____
_____
_____
_____

Weeds Journal

"What I am looking for is not out there, it is in me."
~Helen Keller

Weeds Journal

"Trust the wait. Embrace the uncertainty. Enjoy the beauty of becoming. When nothing is certain, anything is possible."
~Mandy Hale

_____

_____

_____

_____

_____

_____

_____

_____

_____

_____

_____

_____

_____

_____

_____

_____

_____

_____

_____

_____

Practice Pest Control

"People are like dirt. They can either nourish you and help you grow as a person or they can stunt your growth and make you wilt and die."

Plato

Pests are a frequent, yet unwanted, garden visitor. If you've ever planted a garden, or even just had outdoor plants, you know pests can be difficult to deal with. They're often hard to identify, and sometimes it takes multiple attempts, and the frustrating trial and error of different methods, to get rid of them.

The Itsy Bitsy Spider
I had this spider that kept building his web on my hibiscus tree just outside the entryway to my home. He would start the web at my front door, span it across the entryway porch and attach the web to my hibiscus tree for its final leg of support. This became a serious nuisance because the web was in my way every time I tried to enter or leave the house (not to mention I have a ridiculous fear of spiders – they just creep me out). This little spider, that wasn't so little in my mind, was interfering in my daily life. I never knew what I was going to encounter when I opened the front door to leave. Would he be there, waiting for me? How close would he be to the door? When I opened the door would the web break and the spider swing down and land on my head? Would he launch himself at me angrily in protest that I was invading his space? Would he bite me just because he could? (Yes, these ridiculous thoughts went through my head!)

I pondered what to do about the situation. I didn't want to kill the spider. After all, he deserves to live as much as I do and serves a vital role in the ecosystem (i.e., eating those pesky mosquitoes that like to bite me so much). And due to my phobia, there was no way I was going to try to capture and remove him. So I decided to break his web down – in the most glamorous of ways, of course. I grabbed a stick, stood as far away as possible and swatted at the web until it broke, and then ran because, of course, I just knew the spider was going to attack me. When the web came down the spider retreated upward and disappeared. "Good," I thought. "He's gone." But I was sadly mistaken.

The next day when I left the house, there he was. He had rebuilt his web in the same spot and was hanging out right in the middle. So what did I do? Broke the web down again in the same cowardly fashion as the day before. How did he react? The same as before – that perseverant little pest rebuilt. It's like he was taunting me, telling me, "I know I'm in your way and that my presence bothers you, but I don't care. I like it here and I'm not going anywhere."

After about a week and a half of the same song and dance – web goes down, web goes back up – I was on the verge of giving up. I couldn't have this spider that was growing bigger every day (monstrous in my mind) blocking the entry to my front door. I still didn't want to kill him, but I needed a solution. I thought about spraying bug spray in the area without actually spraying him, thinking it would ward him off, but I didn't have any. I was also worried this might kill him. So I decided to break the web one last time in hopes he would retreat and never come back. If he didn't leave, I'd go get some bug spray and give it a whirl. To my surprise, he didn't come back. He finally gave up, realizing he wasn't welcome there and was better suited to set up shop elsewhere. My persistence had paid off, and I was able to remove that pest from my life.

Some pests, like that spider, present an unwelcome presence our lives. That spider was an inconvenience, but he wasn't hurting me. His continued presence, however, would have been an annoyance that added undue stress to my life, which is why I chose to remove him.

Identifying Pests

We all have pests in our lives – people who are annoying and bothersome, some who are more detrimental than others. Many of the pests we encounter are similar to the spider from my story – they disrupt our days, are a source of frustration or annoyance and can even lead us to feel stressed out, sad or angry. The presence of pests in our lives is inevitable. And while we can get rid of some pests, we can't get rid of others. Some of these persistent pests we must learn to coexist with because they're integral parts of our lives (e.g., family members, co-workers, in-laws).

So how do you identify a pest? Much in the same way you would identify a weed. Pay attention to the people you interact and surround yourself with, and take note of how each person makes you feel. Do they lift you up or put you down? Do you feel excited to see them or dread their company? Are you at your best when you're around this person or at your worst? If you dread seeing the person and tend to leave their presence feeling exhausted, stressed, broken, angry or devastated, chances are this person is a pest in your life.

Parasites

Just like there are large and small weeds in life, there are also different types of pests. Parasites are the worst kind –

they feed off of us, eat holes in our mind and spirit and leave us feeling damaged and incomplete, making them the most important pests to get rid of.

What constitutes a parasite? A parasite is someone in your life that takes advantage of and uses you. It's that person whose life always seems to be spiraling out of control and who wants to pull you down the rabbit hole with them. A parasite may be someone who's constantly feeding you a sob story to get money out of you. They may be someone who's always getting into some type of trouble and somehow manages to bring you into it, whether it's to bail them out, provide an alibi, lie for them or implicate you in some way.

No matter what type of parasite you're dealing with, they all have one thing in common – they only seem to call you when they need or want something, and very rarely, if at all, give anything in return. If you find that your relationship is all about the other person and you feel used or neglected, you may be dealing with a parasite.

De-Bug
I learned something interesting when working with clients – they're much more likely to cut toxic foods and substances out of their diet once they're educated about how detrimental these things are to their health, than they are to remove toxic people from their life. They spout a million and one reasons why they can't. Most of the time, the reason is either they don't want to hurt the other person's feelings, or they want to avoid the confrontation. But keeping a toxic person around is just as bad for your mental and emotional

health as a diet filled with toxic foods is to your physical health. In fact, parasites can also affect your physical and spiritual health.

There are several ways to deal with pests and parasites in your life. One method to remove a pest from your life is to slowly break ties with the person. Depending on how complex your relationship is and how adept the person is at rebuilding it, this may require some patience and perseverance on your part.

Start by reducing the amount of communication you have with the person. Less frequent communication on your part signals reduced interest in the relationship. If you don't hear from the other person, there's a good chance that the relationship will naturally run its course and die out.

Another way to sever ties with a pest is to just be candid about it. As we change and mature, so do our relationships. It's the natural order of things to outgrow friends and acquaintances, and it's okay to move on from relationships that are toxic or unfulfilling. Making the decision to leave a friend or acquaintance in your past is never an easy one, but when that person has become a source of stress, pain or sadness, sometimes you just have to tell them goodbye. In this situation, it's best to be honest and upfront about it. Let the person know that this relationship is no longer good for your health or wellbeing, mentally and/or physically, and that you need to move on.

Before going into a conversation such as this, it's important to know what you're going to say and how you're going to say it. Be mindful of the other person's feelings, while still being truthful in the message you're relaying. Make sure you go into the conversation with a clear intention of what you want the outcome to be and be open to listening to their side. The person may not even realize what they're doing or how they're making you feel, especially if you haven't spoken with them about it previously.

If you're concerned about hurting their feelings or saying the wrong thing, consider consulting a trusted friend, family member or professional for advice before talking with the person you want to sever ties with. Keep in mind that it's not always possible to do this without hurting the other person's feelings; in all likelihood, the other person will feel hurt, no matter how gently you put it.

What happens if you try to end a relationship and the person tries to reconnect or rebuild the relationship? This could be a sign that the person truly cares about you and doesn't fully understand how you feel, or is willing to change in order to maintain the relationship. In this case, you need to assess whether or not you want to carry on a relationship with this person. If so, continuing the dialogue in an open and honest way is the first step to improving it. Be clear about what you're feeling and what would need to change in the relationship should you decide to continue it.

Finally, there will be times when you have to learn to coexist with the pests in your life. You obviously don't get to choose your family or even your co-workers, and these may be the people that are causing you strife or inflicting emotional damage. In these cases, you're going to have to identify ways to live with them. One way to do this is to limit your contact with them.

For co-workers that are pests, only communicate with them when necessary and limit your conversations to the business at hand. Make sure the discussion is amicable and professional. You don't have to be friends with all of your co-workers, but you must get along with them and keep a professional demeanor. If you need to work closely with a particular pest, you may have to resort to having an open and honest conversation with the person, similar to what you would have with a friend who has become a pest.

I remember doing just this. I was working as a project manager leading large corporate projects that touched all departments within the company. On one particular project I had to work with a coworker who had become a friend, and he was also dating one of my best friends. We were peers, but in this case, I was his superior. Because I was leading the project, anyone on the project team, regardless of their title or status in the company, reported to me on all things related to the project.

It turned out he didn't like that very much. In group project meetings he would make snarky remarks and efforts to undermine my authority. I didn't understand why or what was going on. I wasn't treating him any differently or calling him out. We were friends, shouldn't he be treating me better than others on the team?

It finally became such an issue that I asked him for a 1-on-1 meeting. He obliged and we sat down to discuss what was going on. It was difficult, but I communicated how his actions were making me feel and asked why he was acting that way. It turned out he didn't even fully realize what he was doing.

As we talked through it, he concluded that he was feeling a little jealous. We both started at the company at the same time and were both on a leadership training track, but I had been promoted to this position and he was feeling a little left behind. The result was him undermining me. I set a clear boundary with him that outside of work we are friends, but when we walk through that door, I have a job to do and I would not tolerate that type of disrespect. After talking it through, he apologized, and the issue never occurred again. Our friendship continued and our relationship improved.

Family is a whole different ball game. When dealing with a difficult family member, don't take it personally (unless you know it is). Let's face it, some people are difficult just for the sake of being difficult, and it may have nothing to do with you – they treat others poorly because of internal reasons. It's important for you to not let them drag you into the mud with them. Whether it's grumpy Uncle Bob or crotchety Aunt Jane, don't add fuel to their flame. Kill them with kindness and just let them be. Say your hellos at family gatherings, be polite and courteous, and then move along to catch up with a relative you enjoy being around.

If it's a close relative you must deal with often, set boundaries. For example, if your mom is constantly telling you how you should be raising your children, let her know that you appreciate her wisdom, but that you have your own methods of childrearing. Ask her to respect your decisions and let her know it's not okay to tell you what to do. If need be, put consequences in place for when the boundary is violated. For example, if your mother still doesn't respect your wishes, you can let her know that every time she tells you how you should raise your children, you will end the conversation and leave the room, which will teach her that her behavior has a negative consequence and will not be tolerated.

If boundaries aren't the issue, you may have to engage in an open and honest discussion about your relationship and how the person is treating you or making you feel. Again, this isn't an easy thing, especially when it comes to family, but if the person is creating undue stress, illness, sadness or pain in your life, it's a necessity for your personal health and wellbeing.

The Art of "No"
Learning to say no to someone is a crucial skill that few possess, but all of us should have. Think back to when
you were a two-year-old. You may not be able to remember that blissful age in your life, but chances are you said the word "no" a lot. And by a lot, I mean all the time. Two-year-olds are notorious for saying no, but then we're taught to be more polite and open to compromise. The problem with this is that many of us forget how powerful and empowering "no" can be and lose our ability to use it. I think it's high time we take a page out of our two-year-old self's playbook and just say "no" more often.

Being able to say no helps to set boundaries and protect you from being taken advantage of. Saying no teaches pests and parasites that they can't benefit from or feed off of you. Think back to the spider I was telling you about. It took repeated efforts of me letting him know he wasn't welcome for him to go away. The same holds true for pests, especially parasites. In most cases, if you keep saying no, they're going to stop asking. And if the relationship is solely an opportunistic one, the person will eventually give up and disappear.

Protect Yourself

Here are some tips to help identify and remove pests and parasites from your life.

Identify and categorize

You can identify people in your life who are pests and parasites by asking yourself the following questions. You don't need to run every person in your life through this list, but if you're questioning a relationship or person you interact with, this is a good place to start. If you can answer yes to any of these questions, there's a chance you have a pest on your hands. The more questions you can answer yes to, the more toxic the person is.

- Does the person only spend time with me as a last resort or when it's convenient for them?
- Do the conversations center around their life, but rarely mine?
- Am I constantly doing favors for them, but when it's their turn to return the favor they're never or rarely able to?
- Do I dread bumping into or seeing this person?

- After spending time with this person, do I feel exhausted, frustrated, sad or anxious in any way?

Once you've identified the pests and parasites in your life, you can begin to take steps to either remove them or mitigate their impact using the techniques previously discussed in this chapter.

Just say no

Learn to exercise your no muscle more! This takes practice. The next time someone asks you to do something that you really don't want to do, don't be afraid to say no. Keep in mind that relationships are give and take, and sometimes we do things we don't necessarily want to do for the sake of the relationship. But when a pest or parasite is constantly looking for assistance or a handout, it's okay to stand up and say no.

Savor Life's Seasons

"Live in each season as it passes; breathe the air,
drink the drink, taste the fruit, and resign yourself
to the influence of the earth."

Henry David Thoreau, Walden

Our planet is miraculous. It's made up of soil, water, vegetation and millions of living, breathing organisms, all of which adapt and change in an effort to thrive on this earth. Seasons are a good example of this.

Depending on where you live in the world, you experience differing degrees of nature's four seasons – winter, spring, summer and fall – and so does the environment around you. The cold of winter brings frost and seeming death to trees, grass and plant life. Streams and lakes freeze over. Many animals lie dormant. Even the sun goes to sleep earlier, leaving the dark to rule the callous, wintery months.

But then something remarkable happens. Spring arrives and brings with it rebirth. Vegetation once thought dead springs to life with new growth. Bodies of water, temporarily frozen solid, thaw. Beasts and tiny critters alike awaken from their slumber with vigor and jump to action in anticipation of the warm months and growing food supplies that lie ahead.

Summer follows shortly thereafter, bringing with it energy, warmth and abundance. Flowers paint the earthen canvas, trees are shrouded in emerald canopies and grass demands regular maintenance. Rivers and streams vibrantly flow. The days are long and the sun shines warmly upon the earth, fueling it with vitality.

Finally, fall descends upon us. Leaves shrivel and tumble from their lofty branches. Squirrels scurry and scavenge for the final bits of food to top off their stores for the barren days ahead. Lakes emit fiery hues of red and orange, reflecting that which is happening around them. Days are cool and crisp, a reminder of the wintry months to come.

Our planet and its occupants adapt to the seasons, finding a way to not only thrive, but to constantly experience growth and rebirth. As inhabitants of this planet, we have learned to adapt to and flourish in our environment. We endure each season with different levels of fervor, waiting in expectation for our favorite to arrive each year.

As humans, we also experience the seasons of life – ups and downs, good days and bad, love and loss. We celebrate achievements, welcome new life and love passionately, but we also grieve death, lament failures and trudge through depression. The important thing to remember is that just as nature's seasons change, so do the seasons of life. It's how we prepare for and get through each season that truly defines us and dictates our growth and happiness.

Winds of Change

I was born and raised in Florida, the land of beautiful white-sand beaches and incessant sunshine. I was made for (and in) Florida, and it lives in me. The warm sun on my skin invigorates me. Crashing waves soothe me. The colors of the sunset, sand and water put me at ease. Yes, I'm a beach baby through and through. I thought I'd never leave my home state, especially for some place cold and snowy, until I was offered an opportunity to advance my career and personal development.

This opportunity was a chance for me to spread my wings and expand my mind, but it required me to leave all of my friends and family behind and move to a place where I knew very few people – three to be exact, one of which would be my new boss. It also came with a big lifestyle change.

First of all, the job was in Rye Brook, NY. "Where's Rye Brook?" you ask. Yeah, that's the same question I had! Rye Brook is a village in Westchester County, NY, about 15 minutes outside of New York City.

Second, I had never lived by myself before, having gone from home to dorms to roommates, and since I didn't really know anyone up north, I was going to be making a real grown-up leap. It would also be a big financial burden to live on my own. Not only would I be solely responsible for all of the bills, the actual cost of living there was about three times higher than Florida.

Finally, I'd be experiencing a huge climate change. Moving from Florida to the greater New York City area meant going from short, mild winters to long, cold, snowy ones.

I had quite a decision to make. First, I looked at all the cons – two friends, cold weather, living on a tight budget, living by myself, snow and ice, family far away, new office, new co-workers, miserably cold, new job, new responsibilities, shorter days, and did I mention, cold!? Then I looked at all the pros – two friends, good job opportunity and increased salary. Not exactly evenly weighted. Nonetheless, I decided to take the job. It was a great opportunity and, as Frederick Douglass said, "If there is no struggle, there is no progress."

I made the move to Stamford, Connecticut which was a short commute to Rye Brook. I chose Stamford because it is coastal and tends to get less snow than inland areas. I found a mother-in-law apartment that was a five-minute walk from the beach, which was a must for this Florida gal. If I was going to leave Florida I was going to be close to the "beach." I put beach in quotes because if you're familiar with the beaches on the Long Island Sound, you know they're not real beaches, especially for someone coming from Florida (sorry if this offends anyone, but I cannot tell a lie). I also liked Stamford because it has a lot of young professionals, and I thought it would be a good place to settle and make some new friends.

The move was exciting – at first. I was fortunate to be able to fly home to Florida often because of work. Projects I was assigned to required me to visit our Florida offices, which afforded me the luxury of seeing all my friends and family often. However, as time went by, my work gradually required me to travel less and less to Florida, making my visits few and far between.

Not long after that things started to go downhill...fast. I was already sad being in a new place far away from everyone I knew and loved, but not being able to visit all the time was the final nail in the proverbial coffin. I was holding on tightly to my life in Florida and that blinded me to the new friends I was making and life that was developing before me. It also made me oblivious to the vast array of things I was learning and the personal growth I was experiencing. I was so focused on everything that I didn't like and leaving my old life behind, that I didn't take the time to see all the good things happening around me.

This led to frustration. Frustration led to sadness. Sadness led to sheer and utter misery. Sure, I went out with my new friends, attended parties and even dated. I put on a brave face, but inside I was far from happy.

With the cost of living so high I was living paycheck to paycheck. There were even months I wasn't quite sure how I was going to pay the bills, especially during the winter months when the oil bill showed up. I had to cut back on a lot and make some tough decisions. I spent a lot of time sitting in my apartment alone, which made it hard for me to meet people and make new friends. This isolation led to weight gain and further sadness and frustration.

Things got even worse when my grandmother became ill and had to have invasive brain surgery. I was sad that I had missed so much precious time with her. I went down for the surgery to be there, but what if something happened to her? I would never be able to forgive myself for missing out on a year of memories.

After one year in Connecticut, I started making plans to go back to Florida. I was sad, broke and cold, and I missed my family. I felt depression setting in and just wanted to go home, so I called my old boss and told him I wanted to come back. He said he'd get to work trying to find me an open position. I didn't renew my lease and found a room for rent living with a woman who seemed super awesome at first, but quickly ended up being a sheer nightmare to live with. I got rid of all my furniture and most of my possessions, with the exception of my bedroom set and whatever would fit in the room I was renting. My new lease even had a 30-day cancellation option – that's how certain I was that I was leaving, no matter what. That's how miserable I was.

After four months of waiting, there were still no open positions in the Florida office. I was told they would either have to create a position for me (which wasn't likely) or I'd have to wait patiently for something to open up. So I waited... and waited... I knew my old boss had my back and was working on it, but I also knew that people very rarely left the company, so I could be waiting a while. My misery and urgency to leave continued to grow with each month. All I could think about was how much I wanted to go back to Florida, how much I wanted to be with my family, but it seemed like God had a different plan for me. He was telling me to hang tight, weather the storm, and better things would come if I could see it through, but I didn't want to.

I decided to take matters into my own hands – instead of waiting for a job at my old office to open up I started applying for new jobs. I was so desperate that I was willing take just about any job as long as it would get me back to Florida. I wasn't thinking about a possible demotion or what it would mean to throw away all the hard work I had done to get where I was in my career. I also wasn't keeping in perspective that I had moved up north for a reason, and leaving to go back to where I was would make it all for nothing.

As I continued to wait for something to pan out, I received a call from a recruiter with a career opportunity that was so great I couldn't pass it up. With this new job came a big bump in pay (something I very much needed to pay off student loan and college debt), title and responsibility, everything I had been working so hard for, and the reason I moved up north to begin with. But there was a drawback — the job was in New York City and accepting it meant I had to settle in here for the long haul.

I finally decided that I needed to get my mind right, stop looking at the negative and start looking at the positive. I would have to make a concerted effort to be happy in my new life, the life I chose by deciding to move up north, the life I would be choosing should I decide to take this new job. I said to myself, "Shannon, if you're going to accept this job, you need to stop wallowing in self-misery. You need to get out of your funk, stop letting life pass you by and make the best of it." At this point in time, I had spent nearly a year and a half going through each day like a robot, missing out on opportunities and failing to relish the moments and people in my life.

When I finally took the blinders off and opened my eyes to what was around me, I realized I had made some great — no, amazing — friends. A few months later I started dating one of those friends, who eventually became my husband and best friend. My career took off; I was sharper and more focused than ever before. Most importantly, I started to enjoy life.

The funny thing is, nothing about my situation had really changed other than the job, which, in all honesty, created longer workdays and higher stress levels for me. **What had really made the impact was changing my way of thinking.** I chose to focus on the good instead of the bad.

Winters were still cold and depressing, but I found a way to tolerate them. I'm not saying I love the snow and cold – I don't. In fact, I very much dislike them (anything below 70 degrees is jacket weather for me). But now I look at the good things winter brings instead of what it takes away – hot soup, wool socks and an excuse to cuddle up on the couch under a fuzzy blanket for a guilt-free, lazy day with my husband, Matt, and our Frenchie, Rover. Winter also became a time for me to slow down and reflect on my life, where I am and where I'm going, without the distraction of the warm summer sun pulling me outside.

I was still far away from my Florida family and friends, but I knew I could visit. I began to open myself up to my new friends and enjoy the positive impact they did and could have on my life. I kept in touch with my Florida friends (and still do) but stopped comparing my new friends to them. They were different and all had a place in my life. As far as my family was concerned, I went to visit as often as I could and talked to them almost daily (also still do). I realized just because I'm physically not there, doesn't mean we can't remain close.

In just that year and a half, I experienced many of life's seasons. A major life change led me to a season of loneliness, longing and the verge of depression. I felt stuck, sad and angry. I experienced regret and fear. But just as the winter ends and spring follows, bringing with it new life and growth, that season in my life ended and was followed with personal evolution and abundance.

As I reflect on that time in my life – one that *seemed* to be one of the most miserable – I realize how grateful I am for enduring it. I learned a lot about myself during that time and harvested tremendous personal growth. That season in my life helped me become stronger, preparing me for much more difficult seasons that I had no idea lay ahead....

A Long, Hard Winter
Five years ago, I lost my best friend and confidant, my dad, to brain cancer. He was only 56 years old when he passed, and it was a sudden and difficult loss. What made it so shocking was that he was strong and healthy. He exercised every day, ate well, and worked outside with his hands. There were no warning signs of what was to come. But I guess with cancer, there seldom are.

It wasn't until my dad passed out one day (which we now know was a seizure) and went to the hospital to be checked out, that we discovered something was wrong. The doctors identified several brain tumors when reviewing his imaging. The diagnosis – Glioblastoma Multiforme Grade IV.

I'll never forget the day I got the call. Matt (my husband) and I had just left church and were going to grab a bite to eat with a friend. We were walking into the restaurant when my sister's name popped up on my caller ID. I knew in my gut something was wrong before she even said a word.

After speaking with her, Matt and I immediately hopped on the train home, and then booked a flight a flight to Florida.

We learned that the tumors were inoperable and growing fast. Despite radiation and chemotherapy, they told us he would only have about 8 to 12 months to live. Within 3 weeks of discovering the tumors, my dad was fully paralyzed on his right (dominant) side and was wheelchair bound. Six and a half months after diagnosis, we lost him.

Nothing can ever prepare you for such a tragic loss. It is something that shapes you as a person and affects every fiber of your being. It becomes a part of you, a load that you carry with you always and in everything. Until I had experienced that type of deep loss, I had no idea what it felt like, and I still have trouble articulating how it affects my every day.

I once used an analogy to help a friend who reached out to me for support after losing his wife to breast cancer a few years after I lost my dad.... He had started a new fitness routine after his wife passed away that entailed him loading up a backpack with weights and walking 3 miles each day. He started with about 30 pounds and worked his way up to 50. At first it was difficult to carry the weight, but the more he walked with it, the easier it got.

I told him that I felt carrying grief was similar to carrying that weighted backpack. The weight never lessens – in fact, it will likely increase over time - but over time you get stronger and the weight gets easier to bear.

In the 5 years since losing my dad, I've had numerous struggles. From launching a tech startup to having a miscarriage and learning we can't have children, to medical issues and losing additional family and friends to cancer, the road has been riddled with potholes, speed bumps and obstacles.

In 2017 I had my appendix removed, a pretty common surgery. Unfortunately, instead of my pain being alleviated afterward, it got increasingly worse over the years – to the point that for an entire 8 months I physically could not sit because it was too painful. I saw every type of doctor and specialist one could think of. I got second and third opinions, was poked and prodded and x-rayed, MRIed and CT scanned, all to no avail.

I kept telling the doctors the reason it was so painful to sit is because it felt like someone was stabbing me with a metal object when I did. They told me they were aware of no such condition that would cause that type of discomfort. And because the doctors couldn't figure out what was inducing so much pain, they fell back on the standard "it must be female problems," it was "all in my head," or - my favorite – "you're just constipated." This resulted in several exploratory surgeries to attempt to find and resolve the issue, none of which helped, and some of which potentially made my pain worse.

Eventually the pain spread from my lower right pelvis to my leg and started to affect my nerves. It began with pins and needles and tingling in my right foot, which ultimately became my entire right leg, hip, groin and buttocks. The pins and needles graduated to include burning, squeezing and electrical shock sensations, as well as feeling like a rubber band was tightening and snapping inside my leg, muscle spasms and the lightest touch feels like sandpaper being rubbed against my skin. Taking a shower is even a nightmare at times because the water will feel like needles raining own on me. I was tested for M.S., Lyme, Lupus and several other auto-immune disorders, none of which I was positive for.

This landed me on a regimen of gabapentin to help control the nerve pain (it only partially helps) and pain killers (I prefer medical marijuana to opioids); not an easy way to live, let alone try to run multiple businesses.

I finally ended up in yet another O.R. for yet another exploratory surgery in 2021. The doctor didn't find anything wrong with me but did find 5 loose titanium surgical staples in my uterus on the lower right-hand side that had been left behind from my appendectomy. Turns out I really **was** being stabbed by a metal object.

After the surgeon removed the staples and I recovered from was my fourth surgery, I was able to sit without feeling like I was being stabbed. Unfortunately, the damage to my nerves had been done (either from the staples directly, the multiple exploratory surgeries or both) and I have now been diagnosed with Complex Regional Pain Syndrome (CRPS), an excruciatingly painful nerve condition for which there is no cure, only pain management.

Sitting continues to be painful for me. In fact, as I write this I am in bed, propped up by pillows with a heating pad under me and my laptop on a cushion on my legs. This condition has affected my work, relationships and ability to enjoy the little things like sitting at the table to enjoy a meal (I eat most of my meals laid back in a recliner).

Despite all of this, I have not given up hope that I will get better and that there are brighter days ahead. People in my life who are aware of my condition ask how I get up every day and work. They wonder how I can remain so positive and upbeat given all I am struggling through. And when someone finds out about my condition and struggles that wasn't previously aware, they are shocked. They often say they would have never known had I not told them and ask how I manage to stay so upbeat and positive given all I'm struggling with. I tell them it's several reasons.

First and foremost, I have an amazing husband, family, friends and community who support me. Second, I believe mindset is a choice. I can choose to feel sorry for myself, wallow and let life pass me by, or I can keep living the best way I am able – I choose to live. Third, as my husband always says, "This is temporary. We'll get through it to brighter days ahead." And while 5 years of pain and suffering doesn't feel temporary, I have faith that I can and will get better.

Why do I open up and share all of this with you? Because I want you to know that you're not alone. My story may not be the same as yours, but we all have struggles and experience the different seasons in life. This is just one season of my life and I believe that there are better ones to come.

Many times, when we're experiencing something difficult, no matter how big or small, it's hard for us to see the forest for the trees. Certain aspects of our lives become so magnified that we have trouble seeing the bigger picture and adjusting our focus, which is exactly what I did after my move – focused on the bad, not seeing all the good. That season taught me a lot and prepared me for the one I'm in now. Because of that experience, I am able to see how my current season, though terrible, equips me to better help others – and I plan to use it to do so.

I've had good seasons and bad throughout my life, with differing levels of impact and lengths of endurance. What I've learned from each is that it <u>will</u> come to an end and a new season <u>will</u> follow; I just have to keep that in perspective and make the best of each and every day.

The Seasons of Life
Everyone experiences life's seasons, you included. How you get through each season is up to you. Will you wallow in the dark and cold of life's winters, or use them as a time of stillness, reflection and contemplation? All of life's seasons bring opportunities; you just have to recognize those moments and take stock in them.

Spring is a season of growth and development, rebirth and hope, purity and renewal. This season could come in the form of new life or a new career, project or idea. It lends an opportunity to invest in your health and wellbeing, make a major change and/or refresh your mind and spirit.

Summer is a season of vitality and light. It's when you're in full bloom, things are going well and you're filled of warmth. Summer presents opportunities for action, openness and taking chances.

Fall is a season of routine. It's a time when things are slowing down or holding steady. The effects of change have settled in and you're reaping the benefits of your hard work. Life is flowing by at a steady, but mellow pace. Fall brings with it time to count your blessings, enjoy your family and friends, and prepare for the winter seasons that may come.

Winter brings dormancy and tranquility. In some cases, this season in life also brings hard times, death, despair, loneliness and depression. But winter also provides you with an opportunity to quiet your mind, reflect on your life, still your soul and contemplate life's lessons.

It's important to remember that all of life's seasons will come and go. Sometimes you may even experience multiple seasons simultaneously. For example, you may be experiencing a dreadful winter in your work life, trudging through each day doing a job you dislike in a toxic environment, while at the same time enjoying life's spring, bursting with anticipation and joy with a budding, new relationship.

There will be times when you're in full bloom, growing faster and burning brighter than you could have ever imagined. It will feel as if you're holding the entire world in the palm of your hand; you're walking on sunshine and cruising by on cloud nine. When you experience this, live in the moment. Take advantage of each and every day and don't take one second for granted. Count and reflect upon your blessings, and share your love and abundance with the world.

Understand that winter will rear its ugly head at times. When this happens, you may feel as if the entire world is crashing down upon you; nothing is going right, everything that can possibly go wrong is going wrong. Use this time for reflection, and take extra care to shift your perspective, knowing that winter will pass and spring will come again, bringing with it rebirth, growth and new opportunities.

Although flowers don't bloom year-round and trees annually lose their leaves, they have learned to endure the harsh seasons and make the most of those they thrive in. You may not always be flourishing , and you will go through periods in life that are steady or dormant. Use these times as opportunities to prepare for and bring forth the seasons of growth that are to come.

Learn to recognize and make the most of the seasons in your life – whether it's watching your children grow into responsible young adults and move off to college, saying goodbye to a relationship you never thought would end, or starting a new career doing what you've always dreamed of – there's something you can take away from every experience.

Winterize

Here are some tips that will help you get through life's winters.

Get your daily dose of sunshine

Keep in mind that negative thoughts and experiences have a much more profound effect on us than positive ones, so making a conscious effort to think positive thoughts and bring good into your life is especially important during times of turbulence or sadness. You'll need a higher dose of sunshine during life's winters to offset and mitigate the negative effects that this season may have.

Keep an eye out for weeds and pests

Weeds and pests tend to invade our lives when we create favorable growing conditions, and during life's winters, it's easy to leave our garden unattended and ripe for them. During hard times, continue to be aware of what is going on not only around, but also within you. This is especially important when you're experiencing hardship, as weeds and pests can have an even more adverse effect than normal (kind of like kicking you when you're down).

Make use of a trellis

Everyone needs a support system – family, friends, mentors and advisors. People in your life who love and support you, and you them, are crucial to your mental, emotional, spiritual and physical wellbeing. In times of sadness and hardship, they're the ones who help hold you up and navigate the rough waters. Trust in them, confide in them and don't be afraid to turn to them for much-needed support.

Weatherproof

Be prepared for the times when life hands you lemons. Sometimes hardship can be predicted; other times it cannot. Regardless, having a plan in place will help you get through the bad days with less bumps and bruises than you would otherwise incur. For example, save funds for a rainy day. You never know when you may lose your job or incur a large, unplanned expense. Having some extra money set aside will help to mitigate the financial burden.

Reflect

Know that spring will come again, so use life's winters as a time to reflect. Ask yourself, what good could possibly come out of this rough patch? What can I learn from this experience? How can I use it to help others? Where do I want to go from here?

Shift your focus

Be solution-focused, not problem-focused. This can be hard, especially when the rain is pouring, but try to focus on solutions to the problem at hand.

Ask yourself what you can do to change your current situation. Determine what is within your control to change and visualize where you want to be. Then set an intention to get there, put a plan in place and execute.

Use the following template to help you gain perspective and become solution-focused.

Issue: What is the problem I'm experiencing?

I can control: What can I control? Forget about what is out of your control; focus on what you have the power to change.

Intended outcome: How do I want the situation to change/what do I want my life to look like? Take a moment to really visualize where you want to be.

My plan: How am I going to reach my intended outcome? Write down the steps for getting there. Be specific and measurable.

Reinforcements: Get out of your own way and remove the excuses. Reinforcements are your backup plans in case something tries to get in your way of accomplishing your goals. Plan for excuses by crafting these statements:

"If [describe obstacle] happens, then I will [describe your backup plan]."

Example:

Issue: I've gained 20 pounds and feel uncomfortable in my own skin. All my clothes are too tight and I'm embarrassed to go out with friends.

I can control: What I eat, how much I exercise, how I feel about myself.

Intended outcome: I will learn to love myself again and improve my self-confidence. I will spend more time with my friends and surround myself with people who love and support me. I will lose the weight I have gained.

My plan: Beginning today, I will improve my diet by eating more whole foods, especially fruits and vegetables. I will eat healthy 80 percent of the time, and not feel bad about treating myself the other 20 percent of the time. I will exercise five times a week for at least 30 minutes. These behaviors/actions will help me lose the weight. I will write in my Sunshine Journal and tell myself at least five confidence-boosting statements every day. I will stop alienating my friends and make an effort to spend time with them.

Reinforcements: If I have a cheat meal, I will not let it sabotage my day or week or plans for success. I will get right back on track and move forward without beating myself up over it. I will plan a "backup" day for working out if I miss one of my planned workout days. If I don't tell myself five good things one day, I will tell myself 10 the next. If I turn down a friend's request to hang out, I will schedule a rain check so that I cannot continue to avoid them.

Now it's your turn! Complete the **Mindset Action Plan** using the worksheet at the end of this chapter. Start small then work your way up to larger, more complex issues once you get the hang of it. Remember to break your goals down into smaller, more manageable milestones as discussed in Chapter 2; and don't forget to **water yourself** to celebrate your achievements!

Mindset Action Plan

Issue:

_____

_____

_____

I can control:

_____

_____

_____

My Plan:

_____

_____

_____

_____

Intended Outcome:

_____

_____

_____

_____

Reinforcements:

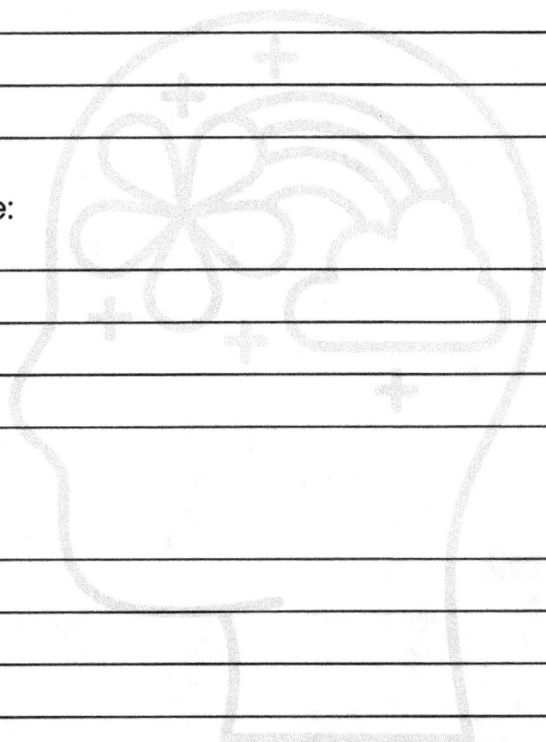

_____

_____

_____

_____

Mindset Action Plan

Issue:

_____

_____

_____

I can control:

_____

_____

_____

My Plan:

_____

_____

_____

_____

Intended Outcome:

_____

_____

_____

_____

Reinforcements:

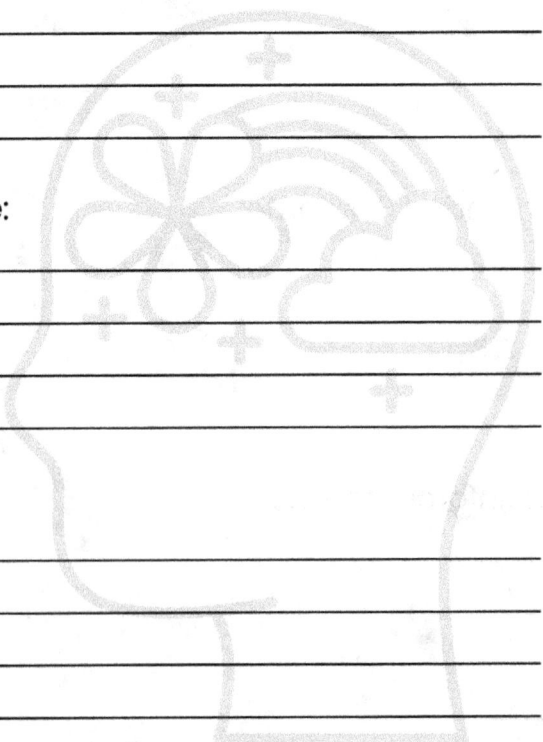

_____

_____

_____

_____

Mindset Action Plan

Issue:

_____

_____

_____

I can control:

_____

_____

_____

My Plan:

_____

_____

_____

_____

Intended Outcome:

_____

_____

_____

_____

Reinforcements:

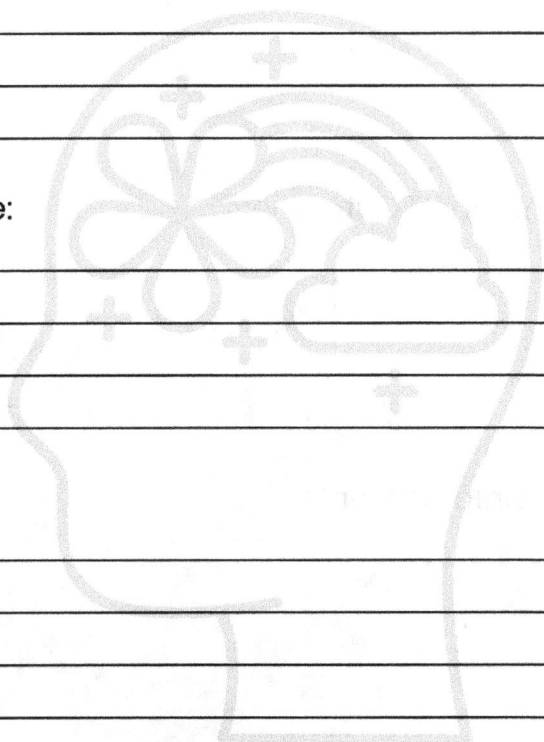

_____

_____

_____

_____

Mindset Action Plan

Issue:

_____

_____

_____

I can control:

_____

_____

_____

My Plan:

_____

_____

_____

_____

Intended Outcome:

_____

_____

_____

_____

Reinforcements:

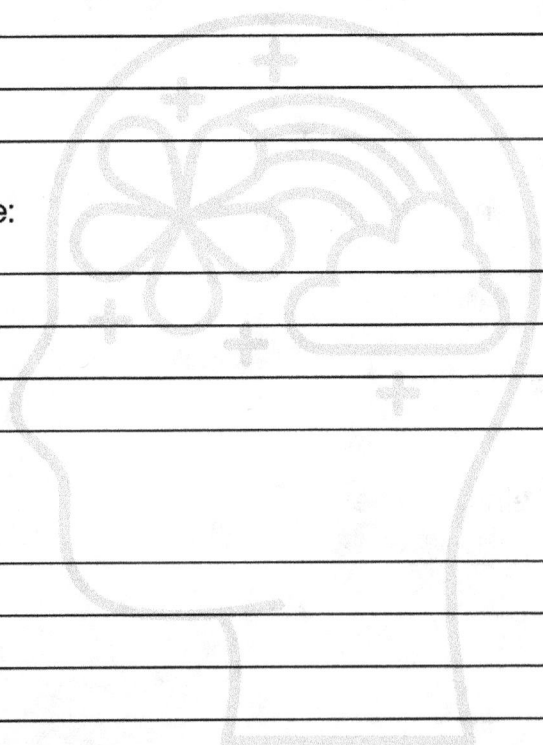

_____

_____

_____

_____

Mindset Action Plan

Issue:

_____

_____

_____

I can control:

_____

_____

_____

My Plan:

_____

_____

_____

_____

Intended Outcome:

_____

_____

_____

_____

Reinforcements:

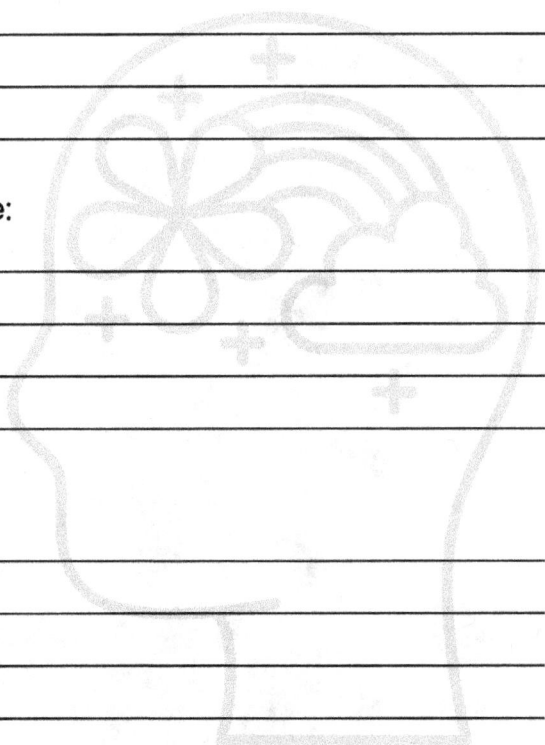

_____

_____

_____

_____

Practice Regular Maintenance

"Happiness resides not in possessions,
and not in gold; happiness dwells in the soul."

Democritus

$\mathcal{T}$o achieve true happiness, one must always work toward it. What do I mean by this? Happiness is a state of mind. It's something that requires conscious effort and work. Being happy isn't something that just happens, nor is it a final destination. Once you have attained happiness, you must continually work to preserve it.

Throughout life you'll experience ups and downs. There will be good days and bad. Improving your life, growing and flourishing are by-products of the effort you put in. The principles in this book will help you achieve growth and live a happy, abundant life, but you can't just perform them once and expect your life to remain harmonious from that point on.

Think about it – you wouldn't plant a seed, water it once, forget about it and then expect it to grow. Nor would you pull a couple of weeds and spray for pests, and then never do either again. If you did, weeds would take over the garden, pests would destroy the leaves and the plants would die of thirst, damage and starvation. To make sure your garden continues to grow and bloom, you would ensure the plants receive ongoing sunlight, water, care and attention. You're no different. Just like that garden, your life requires regular maintenance if you want to continue to experience happiness and wellbeing.

Watering
Starting something new is always fun and exciting. Think about the first time you join a gym. You go for months, fueled by the prospect of the lean, toned body you're going

to get as a result of your efforts. Or when you first start dating someone you really like. You want to see that person all the time and can't seem to get enough of their companionship. How about a new job? You walk in on your first day with your head held high, ready to make your mark. For the first few months, you wake up excited to get to the office and put forth your best. Eventually, however, the novelty wears off, which is perfectly normal.

As much as I hate to say it, the same happens with watering yourself. It'll be a lot of fun at first. You'll be excited and may even count the days until you get to water your plant again because that means you get to do something for yourself. Nevertheless, over time the excitement may wear off and it will become routine; it may even fall to the wayside as your focus shifts to other priorities in life.

It's important to not let that happen. Continual watering is crucial to sustaining your happiness and fueling your personal growth and development. Here are some tips to help keep watering yourself a top priority:

- **Look for new and inventive ways to water yourself.** Don't always water yourself in the same way. This will get stale and reduce the impact that it has. Changing things up will help keep it fun, exciting and fulfilling.
- **Water based on need.** There will be times as you go through life's seasons that you'll need more water and times when you'll need less. Water accordingly, keeping in mind that saturating your life with the wrong types of rewards can be detrimental.

- **Water meaningfully.** Make your watering count! When you water yourself, do more than just reward yourself with a day off or special treat. Yes, these types of watering are good and should be done, but it's important to also water yourself with meaningful experiences that benefit your mind, body and spirit. Doing this will lead to more effective personal growth than simple watering alone.

Letting Your Light Shine

Change your way of thinking and you'll change your life. Don't ever lose sight of that, and always remember that you have control over your own destiny. No matter where you've been, or what you've done, you hold the power to change your tomorrow. As long as you truly believe it, you can do or be anything you dream, but you must think it before you can believe it. And having a support system that believes in and encourages you will go a long way toward helping you achieve your goals. Here are some ways to ensure you continually get sunshine in your life:

- **Keep the shades open.** Don't let your Sunshine Journal fall to the wayside. Sure, it takes a little time and effort to keep up with, but writing down all the good in your life is a great way to remind yourself that there is good in your life. Even if it's not every day, it's important to keep a record of the good so that when the bad seems to take over, you have a place to reference the positive when you can't seem to think about anything but the negative.
- **Let it shine.** Don't stop feeding yourself sunshine. This seems obvious, but it's much easier said than done, especially during hard times. Continue to tell yourself

something positive every day, even when you don't think you need it. Filling yourself up with encouragement and optimism will leave less room for negative and damaging thoughts to take over.

- **Gather up rays.** Look for outside sources of sunshine and soak them up! Spend plenty of time with friends and family members who are supportive and loving and bring out the best in you. Participate in activities that bring you joy. Make time for the people and things in your life that bring you sunshine, and don't let them fall victim to other priorities.

- **Engage in spiritual practice.** Regardless of your personal beliefs, engaging in spirituality can greatly help to increase your overall health and happiness. It's also a valuable source of sunshine. I, for one, have had various levels of spiritual investment throughout my life, and learned that when I fully give my life over to God and speak with Him regularly, I have a much clearer mind, am more at peace and am much happier – even when things aren't necessarily going well. I have also witnessed the power that spirituality has on others. Whether through prayer, meditation or some other form of worship, engaging in spiritual practice will help your light shine bright.

Weeding

Keep weeds in check. The best way to do this is to be mindful of what's happening in your life. Identify new weeds early and pluck them before they have time to take root. This will help to ensure that new weeds don't embed themselves in your life, as they're much harder to control and remove once they've become established.

- **Maintain your Weeds Journal.** When you first begin your Weeds Journal, there's a good chance you'll be writing in it every day. Over time, as you pull weeds from your life and start getting more sunshine, you may not need to utilize it as much. Make sure to always have it on hand, however, and use it on the days when it's needed. Keeping a record of what's causing you strife will help you to identify and pull new weeds as they crop up. It's also therapeutic to get out your negative thoughts and feelings by acknowledging them and writing them down.

- **Log and pull your weeds.** Don't create a Weeds Checklist once and then never come back to it. Practice logging and addressing weeds habitually. I recommend sitting down at regular intervals to look at everything that's going on in your life and record new weeds that may have cropped up. How often you need to do this depends on you. You may need to do it once a month or only twice a year. Whenever you're starting to feel overwhelm and frustration creeping in, that's a good indicator that it's time to log your weeds and address them. If you're having trouble recognizing new weeds, review your Weeds Journal for clues to help you identify them.

Controlling Pests

The people you let into your life can profoundly affect the way in which you live your life. Surround yourself with great people, and you're bound to experience great things. That's why regular pest control is a must. Someone who is a source of sunshine today may become a pest tomorrow, a year from now or even ten years down the road. Don't let them plague you or stunt your growth and development with their negativity.

One way to continually keep pests in check is to companion plant – invest in relationships with friends and family who are positive, supportive and loving. Encircling yourself with good people will help guard you against pests on multiple levels. Not only will your companions help to encourage you and serve as a source of sunshine, they will keep a watchful eye out for pests and warn you when they're invading. In addition, when you're surrounded with good people, the bad stick out much more, making it easier for you to spot and remove the rotten ones.

Change With the Seasons
Seasons change. Keep that in perspective and be prepared to change with them. People and situations around you will change and you will need to be open-minded and able to adjust. Being open to change and ready to adapt to the situation at hand will allow you to make the best of every season in life.

If you need to up your watering, do so. If you need more sunshine to get through dark days, increase your exposure. Whatever it is that you need to do to weather a particular season in life, set an intention and follow through.

When in a season of abundance, enjoy it and don't waste one minute of the joy and happiness you feel. Count every day as a blessing and live life to the fullest. Engage in the practice of gratitude daily. During these periods, take time to plan ahead for seasons that may come. As Forrest Gump said, "Life is like a box of chocolates; you never know what you're gonna get." There's a lot of truth to that, so be prepared to weather an unplanned storm or unexpected hardship. This will mitigate the effects it has on your life.

Changing your way of thinking is also crucial to helping you experience fewer of life's winters. What do I mean by this? Constantly thinking negative thoughts and focusing on the bad will only perpetuate more bad, and you'll end up enduring added winters, even when you should be experiencing summer. I know it's not easy to accept and move on from bad things, or to even change your mindset when suffering through them, but in order to escape winter and move into seasons of growth and happiness, you must learn to do just that.

If you're having trouble shifting your focus and finding a ray of light at the end of a dark tunnel, turn to your family, friends and loved ones for support. They can help bring new perspective to your situation and provide you with love and encouragement, as well as be much-needed sources of sunshine.

Own Your Story

"Owning our story and loving ourselves through that process is the bravest thing that we will ever do."

Brené Brown

The past few years have brought a tidal wave of pain, heartache, loneliness, anxiety and depression in the wake of the Covid-19 Pandemic. Now, more than ever, we need to lean on one another, help our fellow brothers and sisters around the world, lift our voices and share our stories. I've talked with many people who feel alone and isolated, and need a friendly ear, positive voice, and source of inspiration. This was one of the driving factors for me to dust off the original version of this book and revisit the message contained within.

In preparing for the 2nd Edition of this book, I sought to reach beyond my education, research, coaching experience and learnings. I needed to speak with women from across the country; to hear their stories, hopes, fears, dreams and desires. I wanted to understand what they needed most right now.

I interviewed dozens of women (and a man!) over the course of 2 months and saw several clear patterns materialize. The biggest one that stood out for me was **guilt**.

Many women feel guilty taking time for themselves. They want to, and know they need to, but feel that if they have a few extra moments to spare, those should be spent with or doing something for others. Those who were able to overcome this guilt and invest in "me time" and self-care expressed how much healthier and happier they felt. Making time for themselves not only helped their physical, emotional and mental wellbeing, but had a positive impact on their relationships, work and life as a whole.

As a direct result of this guilt, another pattern that arose in my interviews is that **most women are not getting enough "me time."** I said it earlier in this book and I'll say it again...**self-care is NOT selfish.** When you stop to think about it **self-care is actually selfless.** When you make the time to take care of your physical, mental and spiritual health, you are better equipped to take care of others. So when you invest in taking care of yourself, you're also helping others.

Every time you get on a plane, the flight attendants take you through the standard safety instructions, one of which is: if the oxygen masks deploy, put yours on first *then* help the person next to you. Makes sense – if you run out of oxygen and pass out, how are you going to be able to help anyone else? You can't. Self-care is no different. You can't pour from an empty cup. If you never take the time to water yourself (refill your cup), you won't have anything left to give to others.

When I asked the people I interviewed what it is that's keeping them from getting their much needed "me time" I received a variety of answers, but there were a few that stood out amongst most – time, self-imposed pressure and guilt. Since we've already explored guilt, let's look at the others.

Time is our most precious commodity. It's the one thing we can't make more of and can never get back. For those women I interviewed that are now making the time for self-care, that wasn't always the case. They shared that they never used to have the time – not because they didn't have it, but because they weren't making it. They weren't prioritizing themselves. Once they reset their priorities and made the time for themselves, they were thankful they did.

For the majority of women who say they don't have the time for self-care, I'm about to give you a little tough love. Just like those women I interviewed, **you DO have the time, you're just not making it.** You're getting caught up with weeds, pests and parasites, and not flexing your "no" muscle enough. It's time to stop making excuses, reset your priorities and put yourself where you belong, at the top of the list. You are #1 in your life and it's time you start treating yourself like it.

Once you take a long, hard look at your priorities, you may realize that some of that **self-imposed pressure** is unwarranted. As women we have this need to be all things to everyone, and we're often juggling multiple priorities at once – being top mom, the best in our career, a loving wife, supportive daughter, great cook, the list goes on. Guess what, you're only human and there is only one of you.

When you stop to reflect on what is really and truly important to you, you'll likely find that some of the things you were afraid to let go of aren't that important at all. Or maybe they are, but they hold less weight than you once thought. Only then can you release some of that pressure and make room for what's most important – you. You only have one life to live, so live it the fullest!

In the remainder of this chapter, you'll read stories from some of the women I interviewed. These brave women offered to share their stories aspiring to help others. I am so grateful to them for opening up and hope you will be as inspired by their stories as I am.

Stories you'll find in this chapter:

- Stumbling Upon Boundaries by Barb Pritchard
- I Divorced My Sister by April Goff Brown
- "Hello Me!" by Sarah Dziedzic
- Our Mess is Our Message by Mary Ann Pack
- But First, Coffee by Typhanie Winfield-Alexander
- Finding Balance by Rachel Laemle
- Sustaining Self Care by Noelymari S. Velez
- Living Aligned with Passion & Purpose by Lori Raggio
- Honestly "Me" Time by Caitlin Johnson

We ALL have a story to tell. A story that will inspire, uplift and help others. By sharing it you let others know they aren't alone – and find you're not alone - give meaning and context to experiences, and encourage action. Sharing can also be a powerful source of self-discovery and self-healing.

What's your story? I encourage you to share it with the world!

Stumbling Upon Boundaries

Story by Barb Pritchard, Brand Strategist & Intuitive Designer, Infinity Brand Design

Self-care once seemed so alien to me. While every entrepreneurial veteran would impart sage wisdom of its utmost importance, the understanding of one critical concept was especially elusive to me — until I tripped, stumbled, and face planted right into it. The looming, heavy "b" word... Boundaries with a capital B.

In the early days of my full-time business, I fell into the habit most purpose-driven business owners do: saying yes to all-the-things. I was quickly reminded, "Oh hello! I'm still an Introvert!", not that I forgot. Intuition cautioned me that my introverted nature also applied to Zoom calls and energy management was very essential to my well-being.

Wrapping my head around the obscure concept of setting boundaries challenged my hardwired passion to serve. I'm literally here to help! How did this fit into my business? How do I even go about setting them? These seemed like secrets the experts were keeping quiet. Though soon I realized I needed a perspective shift.

Aside from energy, I was reminded that time is my most precious resource and I needed to be a better custodian of it. I followed my inner-knowing and took the first logical step: adjusting my schedule on my Google and booking calendars, only allowing certain times available for calls. I took an assessment of what meetings were healthy for me and/or moving the needle in my business and immediately discontinued anything that wasn't — even if that meant forgoing things I already invested in. Immediately, my shoulders were lighter and I felt I had more room to breathe and create.

My next opportunity for understanding came with using the word "no" and redefining its meaning and feeling. I learned it's ok to stand firm in my "no" and feel zero guilt while still being my usual bubbly, positive self. I was reminded that choices are powerful and, once I came to grips with what I was comfortable with, I could provide options that aligned within those solutions and remove myself from the outcome, even if that meant turning someone away or giving money back to be able to honor the boundaries my heart required.

Boundaries then reminded me that not everything or everyone is meant for a lifetime. You know, the whole reason, season, lifetime adage? In some cases, I realized I'd compartmentalized red flags and who was that helping? In other instances, values or direction no longer aligned. Again, guilt had no place here, nor did long-winded explanations, as I distanced myself from groups and people that no longer felt aligned. I had to just trust intuition and take the leap. I'm grateful I did!

I began my entrepreneurial journey believing Boundaries were heavy, daunting, and unattainable without any real definition. I've since realized they're a necessity to self-care and true growth, both personally and professionally. The path there taught me strength and self-love — I'm no good to anyone on an empty cup. Who knew Boundaries are part-and-parcel to living a light and free life? **I do now.**

I Divorced My Sister

Story by April Goff Brown, Intuitive Journey Guide, Align to You Coaching

I divorced my sister. What???? You can't do that!!! Well, I did. One of my sisters and I have always had a toxic relationship. From our earliest times we were that oil and water that never mixed. From the first time she cut off all my doll's hair at 5 years old! This turmoil became part of our family lore.

It didn't get any better as we got older. We didn't have to really connect or be with each other except at those obligatory family gatherings – you know, holidays and such. Then it got to the point that I was hearing about things that were said. Some of my siblings wondered why she had jealousy, why she didn't like me, and why she fed the fire of dislike to others. I found she had a lot of real estate in my head and I can't tell you how many times I told her off there. She became a bigger presence in my life and I hated it.

Then one day it clicked– if couples could divorce and children could divorce their parents, why couldn't I divorce my sister. My husband was horrified. What it did for me was free up the space she was occupying. I let her go. We were only connected by the accident of birth anyway. She didn't like me any more than I liked her. Making a clear, conscious break was what I needed.

Funny thing, by finally acknowledging it and taking her power over me away, it became easier to accept her. I had no anger, no hate, no love – apathy moved in. The good part about apathy is that it is truly the opposite of love. The more she became nothing to me emotionally, the easier it was to see her not as a sister, but as a person. I found I could begin to appreciate her good points and not focus on the rest.

Years later, we have a respectful, cordial connection. I can care about her as a person while I can keep her at arm's length. She no longer annoys me or vexes me (love that word) or angers me. This is who she is. My divorcing her allowed me to come to a place to accept her in spite of flaws that made me crazy. I allowed myself to make a clean separation between the should and what I needed. No law says I should love her and keep her in my life. Rather, by eliminating the should from the equation, I was able to determine what I could accept and move into that place.

That is healing. I pulled the weeds of should out of my garden of relationships, and planted loving seeds, respectful, seeds, seeds that nurtured my own health that could flourish.

Divorcing my sister was a good thing. It helped the tensions in my birth family. Mostly, though, it helped me and my peace. And in some way, helped us find each other.

"Hello Me!"

Story by Sarah Dziedzic, Owner & Esthetician, Smooth Skin

While I've always cared for myself in certain ways, my journey to better loving and caring for me really began after years of feeling burnt out and walked all over, especially at work, but also by some of the people in my life. I had far too few boundaries, and I felt engulfed in anxiety and depression without really understanding all of the ways it was affecting me at the time.

It took me years to find a therapist I really connected with, but finally finding the right one for me was important, and ended up being really helpful. I still didn't always necessarily love every session in the moment, but some part of me knew there was a bigger picture and that working through my "sh*t" was what I had to do. Some part of me also knew I needed to keep exploring healing modalities.

I decided to try acupuncture next for a multitude of different reasons but in a nutshell, because it seemed like something that could potentially help a number of different things I was dealing with, but without the same long list of side effects as the medications I was on. I went every week for about a year and a half and absolutely loved it. I think this is what made me feel so eager to keep trying other things. Because I was paying fully out of pocket and was getting ready to move out of my parents', I did eventually stop, but I was already getting into other modalities and felt much better than when I'd started, so I was alright with it.

Reiki is another one that I'd tried years prior when I was in school for esthetics, and I knew it was something I wanted to learn for myself at some point. Years later, a co-worker (now friend) at a salon I was working at was also a reiki master, and she gave me the contact information for the woman who trained her. I reached out and we talked for a while, and she told me she would teach me, but asked if I'd be open to some "life coaching" sessions first, because she felt it would really make a difference. That was an understatement.

It didn't all happen right then and there, but those sessions changed everything for me. I kind of felt like a new person. Even people close to me eventually started noticing beautiful changes. And that really was just the very beginning. What followed has led to the absolute best version of myself, and it's only been a few (maybe a little more than a few) years.

Get to know yourself. And then learn to love every single part of yourself. Your physical body, of course, but also (and mostly) everything else that makes you, you. It isn't an easy journey, but I think you'll find it's one of the most important things you'll ever do.

Our Mess is our Message

Story by Mary Ann Pack, Author & Publisher, Envision Greatness, LLC & Press

As a child of religious trauma, I grew up believing so many lies about who I really was. I was told how unworthy and sinful I was. That I should be ashamed and beg for forgiveness from an angry god. If I followed the rules and obeyed the dogma, then god would smile upon me. If I disobeyed, I was condemned to eternal damnation. Lovely for a child to deal with!

There was so much tension and fear in my little body that I began getting sick as a child, and my body continued to deteriorate throughout my adulthood. My life was filled with anger and fear, which my body expressed as illness and disease, requiring drugs and surgeries.

By my mid-30s, my body crashed, and I sought alternative healing in nutritional and herbal supplements. What a joy to find relief! That experience led me to other alternative healing practices such as energy work, crystals, feng shui, light work, and sound healing. All taboo within the church, so I studied in secret for years.

Studying alternative healing methods opened my eyes to evaluate my beliefs. The study of metaphysics let me know that the emotional trauma I suffered caused my body to reject that energy and create illnesses. Once I began to find relief by releasing beliefs that felt so bad to my soul, I continued to heal and feel whole.

I finally left the church in my mid-40s and never looked back. I lost all of my friends and some of my family members. But I had ME! I was beginning to love and trust my own inner guidance. I called in teachers and mentors to help me find a new spiritual path! They didn't tell me what to believe they simply pointed me to my own guidance within. From within came my new beliefs that my soul could trust.

My absolute favorite Abraham-Hicks quote that changed my life was, "You are joy looking for a way to express." When I heard that for the first time, my soul lept for joy! My soul recognized 141tself! And I recognized who I really was for the first time in my life!

As I always say, our mess is our message! The mess I transformed through has become my message. I've been freed to unmute my voice through my writing, publishing books for myself and others, and podcasting. I love sharing the stories of the victorious sovereigns who are now living in joyous thriving!

My mission is now to spread more love and joy around the globe. Let's write the world happy, one word at a time!

But First, Coffee

Story by Typhanie Winfield-Alexander, Holistic Life Coach & Personal Development Specialist, Momentum Life Mastery Coaching, LLC

4:02 am. I can't remember the exact day or even which season. Sitting there, in the dark drinking my first morning cup of hot coffee (French vanilla light & sweet) I just remember thinking, "This isn't working..."

Some time ago, I took a long hard look at my life. I was not happy with where I was going and felt like I had wasted SO much time. At first, all I could think about was the "coulda, shoulda & wouldas". If only I had done things differently, maybe we wouldn't be struggling. Maybe we'd be able to finance our creative ideas, maybe we'd own our home instead of renting for (too many to mention) years.
SO many emotions. Fear, hurt, shame, you name it, I felt it.

After rewarming my coffee for at least the third time (#momlife), a few things happened:

First, I realized that not only did I WANT better, I FINALLY considered that maybe, JUST maybe I DESERVED better. It was time for me to accept responsibility for my part my actions or inactions had in leading to my circumstances and CHOOSE my path forward.

Next, after floating the idea for months, I decided to pursue my heart-work and become certified as a life coach. You see, I'd been an early childhood professional for two decades. Helping and mentoring others was already a significant part of my life, but it was informal, unfocused and if we're being honest, unhealthy to "coach" others without the necessary tools to protect your energy and stay grounded. Sidebar: When you begin the certification process, you WILL face your fears, shadows & traumas (be warned... they don't tell you THAT part in the brochure!).

The truth is, I could not be more grateful for the experience to be broken down and reconstructed! I not only found my passion, but I started to heal my own root issues (ESPECIALLY those around finances and my "money story"). Working on self-care, work-life alignment, improved eating habits, relationships, even better SLEEP were ALL part of the process. I was on a ROLL! I was finally ready to tackle those pesky finances and "change my life"...

The most pivotal moment for me happened when I waltzed my way into a "big" bank with my $500 in cash and my "new-found" confidence to open a SECURED credit card. I thought this would be a perfect way to start rebuilding my abysmal credit.

I was DENIED. What?!! I was devastated. I couldn't understand it. How could I be denied with CASH-in-HAND?!! Well, as it turns out, I had shifted my thinking but not my behavior. I'd skipped some CRITICAL action steps. There were things that I needed to address that required me to do some honest work around my choices. I simply wasn't ready (yet).

That is when things got serious, y'all.

I got laser focused on implementing customized action steps (a process I now call the A.R.R.O.W method) to set, attain & maintain goals. This framework became the foundation of my signature programs, Di$cipline Work$ - Masterclass" & "Roots to Results – Group Coaching Program". (Shameless plug- Hey, the system works!)

Fast forward less than two years later... The same bank that originally denied my application for $500 secured credit card approved my application for a mortgage and my FIRST home purchase. At age 52, I finally understood the connection between my choices and how they create the changes I desire and deserve.

I invite and challenge you to begin the journey towards achieving your big goal. Take a moment to reflect:
- What do I truly need to bring my life into alignment.
- What do I really want?
- Why does it matter?
- What is the cost of NOT trying?

I know it gets hard. I know you get tired. Sometimes we feel like the more we try to create the life we want the more obstacles are on our path. You don't have to be perfect. You don't have to go quickly, and you CERTAINLY don't have to walk this journey alone. Remember that your choices create changes. You get to decide how to move forward. Take a breath, Get organized, gather resources, create time and space and, most importantly, DO the work...

But first, coffee!

Finding Balance

Story by Rachel Laemle, R.D. to be...

As a young girl with many passions and a world to explore, I attended a large university to cater all my interests: cooking, fitness, gardening, Greek life, art, and more. I was ready to show up and join 15+ clubs, meet new people, and create the life I dreamed of. Then the pandemic hit.

Freshman year was mostly a dorm quarantine: an engaged student's nightmare. Beginning college online with a burning desire to get my hands dirty, I joined anything offered virtually. Managing to stay busy and make many friends, I had a successful start.

Sophomore year brought face-to-face opportunities and rigorous classes, but also stress and realizing that 24 hours is not enough time in the day. Barely seeing my closest friends, squeezing 30-minute workouts in between activities, and finessing homework at midnight, nothing got my 100%. The social and academic impact prevented me from seeing my true self each day and from enjoying little moments. I was always thinking about the next place to run. Physical and visible stress habits also emerged, which I did not prioritize on the endless to do list. This lifestyle dragged me down for a year. The college life I envisioned had become a speedy and hectic blur.

Summer break was a great reset before junior year. I studied abroad for six weeks and made great friends, learned a new culture and ate great food. Everything I wished for had come true! But, returning to a normal

145

semester concluded in quickly hitting rock bottom. The lack of self-care from Spring continued into the Fall and became visible to family and friends, including extracurricular groups that reached out about lack of attendance.

I began the only option: dropping things. I sent one apology message after another about having overcommitted myself. In midweek tears early Fall, I took a few days at home to find myself. I thought about priorities and values, then arrived back to campus all fresh.

The next few weeks included two hours per day in the gym and cooking dinner with friends. I was extremely happier in those shoes. Sometimes I felt like a slacker with time on my hands to enjoy things, but this schedule showed me what a normalized routine feels like, and that no person is built to do everything.

While I have yet to find the perfect balance between academic, social, extracurricular, and most importantly self-care, I am entering Spring of my junior year with a healthier and more aware mindset. Those I surround myself with know of my lowest point and check in on my progress. Every second with friends is cherished and only positive places are taken up upon. I am comfortable saying 'no' by feeling less pressure to attend everything that's offered. This brings me happiness and expresses the capability of self-control. For the rest of life, I have learned to explore one adventure at a time with my all and true self.

Sustaining Self Care

Story by Noelymari S. Velez of JCV Freelance Photography, LLC

In my life I have realized the importance of self-care, a time I get to nurture myself and get to know who I am. This has changed my life because it has helped me understand that if I am not well, I can't take care of others. My spiritual well-being is also as important as any other routines that I have created.

I have learned to prioritize 'me time' by scheduling it and making it a point to add this time to my calendar. This dedicated time is as important as making time to for a business meeting, to eat and sleep. I have created an environment in my life where I can nourish my soul by reading, getting closer to God, nourishing my body and staying active.

I realized that when I feel happy and I am not experiencing any aches or pains, I feel my best. One of the things that have helped me accomplish this is to schedule monthly 30-minute massages to my self-care routine. This allows me to relax, connect with any aches that I may be feeling and how to release them.

As many experienced, the pandemic in 2020 and beyond has not been easy on how our daily routines were disturbed. We had no idea how things were going to be from one day to the other. Routines were broken and we couldn't sustain a rhythm, balancing our work, small business, and personal life. Often my husband and I tried to create a rhythm of self-care, but found it was hard to maintain.

At the beginning of 2023, my husband and I decided to get back on track with our health. We joined a health and wellness program that has re-focused us to eating healthy and getting back into a workout routine. These workouts are scheduled just like my massages where I ensure they are not missed.

Having a positive and 'can do' attitude will take you far. Having confidence in yourself and creating your own narrative, you can accomplish anything. Create an environment around you that you are proud of where you carry yourself in a way that no one can take away your sunshine. Continue to create healthy habits and sustaining your self-care routines without feeling guilty. These will help you from the inside out.

Living Aligned with Passion & Purpose

Story by Lori Raggio, Founder & CEO of Inspire Greatness Coaching & Conssulting LLC

Seeking spiritual connection after a 32-year marriage ended, I listened to my heart and soul's calling and moved from Maryland to Arizona at the height of a global pandemic. My East coast friends say the desert is so brown and dead, but I assure you it is teeming with life. The nourishment my body needed was perpetual sun, warmth and the groundedness of the mountains and desert.

I have a continuous stream of life force energy that I use intentionally with discernment and trust my own pace. I have found and unmuted my voice and I take a bold stand for other women to do the same.

Now, my self-care is focused on physical, emotional, spiritual, and geographical health. I created the geographical soulmate which is the location(s) where our heart and soul have called us to visit and/or live where we are nurtured to show up as our greatest self. Anything and everything is possible in these soul places and the connection with the land supports us in designing the life we desire and deserve. In Arizona my life has profoundly changed, I have found my Why, How and What, and I support my clients in finding theirs.

Why: Better Way
I believe there are always better ways to do and be, opportunities, and possibilities to get outside our comfort

zone, explore and experiment to discover a new expanded version of ourselves.

How: Mastery
As a lifelong learner, acquirer of continuous knowledge and Sourced experiences, I partner with my clients in seeing beyond the superficial surface, beyond their masks, glitz, and glitter, and speaking about their truth by digging deep and unmuting their voice.

What: Trust
I create a consistent, safe, and trusting space so that a relationship is built quickly, leading to growth. I hold space for talking about desires and discomfort, and I challenge my clients about their limiting beliefs so that massive transformation can occur.

I have learned that:
- Workaholism is not a badge of honor
- Worthiness is our birthright, not dependent on overdoing and overachieving
- Suffering is not a rite of passage or a prerequisite for joy and success
- Intentional focus of time and energy on what we desire most requires us to surrender to the divine to unveil the magic
- We are not alone
- Becoming is not a destination, it is a spiritual journey

Now, authenticity, integrity, vulnerability, and trust are the foundational nutrients that support me in living a life of co-creation, connection, community, and collaboration.

I am a catalyst for truth, a disruptor, change agent, an energy first transformational leader who embodies leadership that is spirit inspired, compassion driven and intuitively executed.

I am powered by purpose, driven by insatiable curiosity, and guided by Source to partner with women leaders/ entrepreneurs to remove their armor, stop being a spectator on the side lines living by default, and take bold courageous steps to live aligned with their passion and purpose while intentionally becoming the leader the world needs now.

Honestly "Me" Time

Story by Caitlin Johnson, Founder of Bold-Bird Consulting

I discovered early on that the best time to implement "Me Time" was in the very early morning. In the early morning, my kids aren't awake yet and work demands haven't kicked in yet. For over a decade, I have started my day at 5:00am and generally have about two hours to invest in my emotional, mental, and physical self.

My morning routine starts with sitting on the floor with a cup of coffee and a notebook. For the first 30-45 minutes, I allow myself to peacefully and slowly wake up. I choose to sit on the floor so that I can stretch and warm up for the day. Once my coffee kicks-in, I start thinking and brainstorming ideas! It's my favorite time of the morning as the ideas are always so motivating and exciting! I'll write in my notebook reflections from the previous day, I may start a small to-do list, or I may dive into an innovative idea for my business.

This thought and reflection time is critical for me to stop and process the previous day's activities. I like to look at what went well and how can I repeat it as well as what opportunities presented themselves and how can I adjust or course correct. Without this reflective time, I find I get too caught up in the day-to-day and I get absorbed in just reacting rather than proactively managing my day. This is an opportunity to clear my head and gain clarity.

After this reflective note-taking and journaling, I'll switch gears and go to the gym or do a home workout. Another strategy that works really well for me in investing in 'Me Time' is training for a race of some sort. I love the challenge behind training for a triathlon such as an Ironman. Now, I understand training for an event like this isn't everyone's cup of tea. However, over the years, I have discovered that I'm innately a high performer and I enjoy achieving different challenges. It motivates ME, and that's what's important! Training has become a meditative activity for me. Swimming, running, and cycling allow me to zone out, and I can transcend past the activity and into a state of joy.

It's taken me some time to identify the best way to take care of myself, lots of trial and error. I'm not one that enjoys long baths...I need to be active. The most important part of self-care to me is being honest with myself in identifying my needs and trying not to compare myself to everyone else. I focus on discovering what energizes me and stick to it. Even if that means waking up at 5am and completing an Ironman!

Happily Ever After

"Happily ever after is not a fairy tale. It's a choice."

Fawn Weaver

I'm sure you're wondering what happened to that beautiful and talented woman I was telling you about at the beginning of the book. I'm happy to say that she is no longer experiencing anxiety and is sleeping much better at night. She and her ex-husband nurtured a healthy friendship that brought them back together, and she is giving her son the upbringing she had hoped for. In addition, she has taken her business to the next level and is sharing her talents with the world.

Her life isn't perfect. She continually works to improve her confidence, self-esteem and overall happiness, but she has transformed tremendously as a result of employing the principles in this book. And I have gained an amazing friend.

Final Note

I hope that you have found the principles in this book helpful and easy to implement. I truly believe that if you make more time for and invest in yourself, get more sunshine, weed out the bad and shift your thoughts and perspective, you can live the life you've always dreamed of.

My wish for you is that you have a life filled with health, happiness and abundance, and that all of your dreams come true. You are beautiful, strong and worthy of all of the treasures that life has to offer – love, friendship, joy, wellbeing, accomplishment and so much more! Now it's time for you to believe it and take control of your destiny so you can thrive.

Acknowledgements

I would like to thank the many people without whom this book would not be possible.

First and foremost, I would like to thank my husband, Matt, who has believed in and supported my dreams, even when they seemed outlandish. Matt, you have been my rock and have not wavered despite the many hardships we have endured throughout the years. You always help me to remember that adversity is just temporary and there is light at the end of the tunnel. I love dancing in the sunshine with you and am so glad I get to do life with you, my best friend and soul mate.

I would like to thank my amazing family for always encouraging and supporting me. I am truly blessed to have such a wonderful family – I love you all more than words can say. I'd like to give special thanks to my Nene who has taught me so much and inspired me in numerous ways. Thank you for letting me "live history" with you and for your tremendous love and guidance. To my nephew, Patrick, thank you for bringing so much joy to our lives. You are special beyond measure.

To my dad, although you are no longer on this earth to see how both I and this book have evolved, I know your spirit is with me. I can feel you by my side, holding my hand, encouraging me, believing in me and lighting my way to a brighter future.

To my wonderful editor, Lauren Fetterman (the BEST editor in the world), thank you for pushing me to look outside the box and shift the perspective with which I see my words. Because of you, this book is infinitely better than it could have ever been had I ventured out on my own. I know no "i" will ever go undotted, nor any "t" ever go uncrossed with you on my team.

To the beautiful princess who inspired this book (you know who you are), thank you for your trust and illumination. It is because of you that Water Yourself was even born. Thank you for allowing me to share your story with the world. Always believe in yourself and your talents. You are a beautiful person, inside an out.

To my dear friends Bree and Hezz, thank you for your countless years of irreplaceable friendship. You will always hold a special place in my heart no matter how much space or time comes between us. And to Bree, thank you for the original cover design of this book. Your vision, talent and creativity made for the perfect balance of color and imagery to dress the message within.

To my bestie, Nichole, thank you for your support in all things big and small. Your big heart and beautiful soul sparkle. You bring joy and happiness to those who know you and inspire healing through your kindness. I am so appreciative to have you in my life. Thank you for your unending love and support. Love you girlie!

Everyone needs a village to support them, and I am so humbled and blessed to have an incredible community of friends and supporters who have encouraged and championed me over the years. To Zef, my SOW sister, thanks for being a part of my world and for your boundless energy. Thank you to Dr. Jacqueline King for believing in Water Yourself and providing it with a new platform to transform lives. To my SOW Sisters and LPL tribe, especially Dr. Davia Shepherd, you have all taught me so much and I am blessed to have friends like you. To all those who have been there through this journey and advocated my dreams: Momma and Poppa D, the Malkin and Daniels families, Alex Virvo, Rodger Gibson, Jon Winkel, Stacey Cohen, Kathy D'Agostino and countless others. And a special thanks to my right hand, Megan Golez, without whom I wouldn't be able to accomplish all I need to.

I would like to give special thanks to all those who took the time out of their busy lives to share their stories of self-care with me for this book: Barb Pritchard, April Goff Brown, Sarah Dziedzic, Mary Ann Pack, Typhanie Winfield-Alexander, Rachel Laemle, Noelymari S. Velez, Lori Raggio and Caitlin Johnson.

Finally, I can't go without thanking God for your unconditional love and blessings.

References

1. Butler-Bowdon, Tom. *50 Psychology Classics: Who We Are, How We Think, What We Do: Insight and Inspiration from 50 Key Books.* New York: MJF, 2007. Print.

2. Damerow, Gail. "14 Ways to Extend Your Growing Season." Mother Earth News. N.p., n.d. Web.

3. Emoto, Masaru, and David A. Thayne. *The Miracle of Water.* New York: Atria, 2011. Print.

4. Emoto, Masaru. *The Hidden Messages in Water.* Hillsboro, Or.: Beyond Words Pub., 2004. Print.

5. Grant/CNBC, Kelli B. "Americans Hate Their Jobs, Even With Perks." USAtoday.com. A Gannett Company, 30 June 2013. Web.

6. Holmes, Roger, and Eleanore Lewis. *The Beginners' Guide to Gardening.* Upper Saddle River, NJ: Creative Homeowner, 2013. Print.

7. Masaru Emoto's Rice Experiment. YouTube. TheBizLife, 29 Mar. 2010. Web. 2014.

8. Maslow, Abraham H. *A Theory of Human Motivation.* Mansfield Centre: Martino, 2013. Print.

9. "STRESS...At Work." Centers for Disease Control and Prevention. Centers for Disease Control and Prevention, 06 June 2014. Web.

10. "Unit 1." Communicating from the Inside Out. N.p.: Kendall Hunt Pub, 2008. 43-45. Print.

11. Waldman, Mark, and Andrew Newberg, MD. "The Most Dangerous Word in the World." Psychology Today. N.p., 01 Aug. 2012. Web.

12. *Happy.* Directed by Roko Belic, narrated by Marci Shimoff. 2011.

13. Putnam, Robert D. *Bowling Alone: The Collapse and Revival of American Community.* New York: Simon & Schuster, 2000. Print.

14. The Gallup Organization. Washington, D.C. *State of the Global Workplace: 2022 Report.* Web.

About the Author

Shannon Malkin Daniels is a communication nerd, entrepreneur, author, Forty Under 40 and TEDx speaker who views obstacles as opportunities and believes anything is possible with the right combination of creativity, hard work and perseverance. Applying this mindset has enabled Shannon to develop innovative solutions and stand out as a leader.

Shannon holds a master's in interpersonal communication from the University of Central Florida and has served on the faculty at Columbia University and Iona College. She is also a Certified Holistic Health Coach and is board certified by the American Association of Drugless Practitioners as a Holistic Health Practitioner. Shannon obtained her Health Coach certification from the Institute for Integrative Nutrition, where she studied more than 100 dietary theories, practical lifestyle management techniques and innovative coaching methods with some of the world's top health and wellness experts.

For nearly a decade Shannon has been helping people unlock their potential and become more confident communicators as a public speaking, communication and confidence coach. Frustrated with the lack of engagement and measurement presentation technologies provided, she founded encaptiv in 2018, an award-winning audience engagement and conversion platform for virtual, hybrid and in-person presentations and events.

Shannon is the Co-Founder of SOW Victory Fest, a global event that celebrates, elevates and empowers women. She is also Co-Founder of Stamford Innovation Week, a week-long festival and conference celebrating innovation, entrepreneurship and technology.

Shannon was born and raised in Florida, and moved to the Northeast in 2008 where she met her husband, Matt. They love the outdoors, going to the beach, hiking, biking and spending time with their French Bulldog, Rover.

Connect with Shannon online at:

shannonmalkindaniels.com

Twitter: @shannonmdaniels
LinkedIn: /shannonmalkindaniels
Facebook: /shannonmdaniels
Instagram: @shannonmdaniels